Vegan

CAMPER VAN COOKING

SIMPLE AND HEALTHY RECIPES
FOR COOKING ANYTIME ANYWHERE
ON TWO HOTPLATES

ANINA GEPP

GRUB STREET • LONDON

Published in 2023 by
Grub Street
4 Rainham Close
London
SWII 6SS

Email: food@grubstreet.co.uk
Web: www.grubstreet.co.uk
Twitter: @grub_street
Facebook: Grub Street Publishing

Published originally in German as *Vantastic Kitchen*

Photography: Anina Gepp and Christian Jäger
Photograph location index
Page 4 Castel del Piano, Italy
Page 17 Osterøy, Norway
Page 22 Sandnes, Norway
Page and cover design: Myriam Bell Design, UK

A CIP catalogue record for this book is available from the British Library.

ISBN 978-I-911667-85-8

Printed and bound by Finidr, Czech Republic.

CONTENTS

TAKING THE PLUNGE: WHY WE SWAPPED OUR FLAT FOR A CAMPER VAN

When we tell the people we meet on the road that the 'bus' they're looking at is our home, the usual reaction is disbelief. Of course, van life has become a fashionable topic, and holidaying in a camper van is now a trendy thing to do. But giving up a whole flat and moving into a six-square-metre space with only the bare essentials is something very few people can picture themselves doing. And to be honest, until a few years ago, I wouldn't have been one of them. Even the thought of a holiday in accommodation you took everywhere with you hadn't crossed my mind. But that was all soon to change.

Unlike me, my partner Chris had long been familiar with camper vans. Even as a child, he would spend the summer holidays with his family travelling around in a Volkswagen Bus camper van. So, it was obvious that he should want to show me this world that was so foreign to me. I was persuaded to at least give it a chance. We agreed on three weeks in Spain and Portugal. Sun, beach and sea. I thought it might be something I could handle in warm and sunny weather.

Then something happened that neither Chris nor I could have imagined: I fell head over heels in love with van life, on the very first evening. I was blown away by the experience of falling asleep with a view of the sunset and the sea — and also waking up with the sun. It was amazing how quickly I was able to switch off, given that I would typically still be churning things over in my head, even after being on holiday for several days. I slept better than ever in the roof tent of our hired camper van, and I enjoyed making my morning coffee in the espresso maker and unrolling the yoga mat while still in my pyjamas. Naturally, it was very cramped inside the van, and it got messy very quickly, but it didn't matter when you had the big wide world for a living room; and

MINIMALIST COOKING FOR THE MAXIMUM FLAVOUR

This cookbook is not only meant to accompany you on your travels but also has its place in your kitchen at home. The reason for this is that given our hectic everyday lives, we all need a little more simplicity. Through eighty or so recipes in *Vegan Camper Van Cooking*, my goal is to show you that a healthy, balanced and sustainable diet need not be overly elaborate or particularly time-consuming.

My cookbook is for anybody who wants more variety and fresh food in their diet without having to spend hours in the kitchen. Whether at home or on the road, these everyday recipes make use of local and seasonal ingredients that are easy to source, and they are suitable for both novice cooks and more adventurous foodies.

The big challenge in a camper van kitchen is to bring the same amount of flavour, sophistication and variety to the plate in a much smaller space. Instead of four hobs, my gas cooker only has two, and I need one of them to operate my stovetop oven. What might sound complicated at first is actually a blessing. Space constraints made me think about how I could cleverly simplify, modify and even reinvent dishes. As a result, I don't see cooking in a van as a restriction, but rather as a rewarding experience. Not only are the simple dishes often the best, but they can also be elevated with just a few tricks and flourishes; it always amazes me that they work so well in such a small space.

The special thing about the recipes in my book is that they can be customised. Almost every recipe comes with tips on how to enhance and/or expand it. That way, there's something for everyone: for those who want to quickly whip up something delicious after work, and for those who prefer to take more time to experiment when they cook and are always on the lookout for new flavour combinations and experiences. Either way, healthy and wholesome dishes to prepare quickly and with few ingredients are essential both when travelling and at home.

All the dishes in this book — as in my first cookbook *Eat Your Greens!* — are purely

plant-based. No animal products are used. Once again, this second book focuses on sustainability. As such, the recipes make use of the ingredients that can be bought locally and seasonally in the respective countries. I source my ingredients from farmers' markets and organic and zero-waste shops in the countries I visit. I've also been inspired by visits to restaurants and the people I've met along the way.

So, as well as fresh ingredients, many personal stories always end up in the cooking pot, which gives the dishes a very special touch and add food for thought, whether on the road or at home.

MY FOUR-WHEELED KITCHEN
Essentially, I have a fully-equipped kitchen, which means that I don't have to make do without all the conveniences that you have at home. Of course, there are also differences here and there, which I'll explain to you in this chapter. Now I'll take you on a tour of my domain, the heart of our van.

GAS AND ELECTRICITY
As I mentioned earlier, I cook on two hobs instead of four. And unlike in many flats, I cook with gas. Everything else is powered by the electricity generated by the solar panels on our roof. That's enough to operate the eighty-litre fridge with a small freezer compartment, and it supplies a power point that even allows me to plug in my blender.

WATER SUPPLY
All the washing is done by hand in cold water. The dirty water drains into a tank under the sink, where it collects until we can empty it at the nearest waste-water disposal point.

The water from the tap is perfectly fine for drinking as we filter it first time when we fill the water tank, and then it goes through a second filter located under the sink. This saves us the hassle of having to store bottles, and it's more sustainable than constantly having to buy spring water. The water tank holds a total of 100 litres of fresh water, but this amount serves both our kitchen and our outdoor shower. This alone is a very good reason for the strict management of this valuable resource.

ORGANISATION AND STORAGE
Speaking of valuable resources, water isn't the only commodity in limited supply. The main limitation with a camper van is, naturally, space. Our kitchen has three large drawers where we store cutlery, bowls, plates, cups, pots and pans, and all the coffee-making equipment, among many others. There are two cupboards: one on the left and the other on the right of the drawers. The one on the right, under the sink, is where the refuse bin is kept, and the one on the left holds the gas bottle, with some space to store food. As you can imagine, the one cupboard isn't enough for all the food. That's why we have compartments concealed under the front cab seats that serve as our store-cupboard for essential supplies. Things that aren't needed every day are kept in the back of the van. There — in what is an excuse for a boot — there's still room for non-perishable items that can be stored for a long time.

We store fresh food — fruit and vegetables — in wide-mesh hanging nets in the kitchen. That way we can always see what we have left, and so we don't stow perishable items in places where we forget about them. A striking feature of our van kitchen is the set of jars we secured to the ceiling over the sink. They contain all the toppings that we like to put on our morning porridge or muesli.

OVEN

What would a cookbook be without oven dishes? Fortunately, there's also a great solution for this. The Omnia is an oven that I use on the hob of my gas cooker that works like the conventional oven you have at home. It does look a little different though, and it takes a little practice before all the dishes turn out exactly the way you're used to seeing them. But once you get the hang of it, it's hard to imagine a camper van kitchen without an Omnia. I've devised all sorts of dishes in it for this book, including lasagne, focaccia, muffins and moussaka. Anything is possible. To make it easier for you to follow, each oven recipe comes with two sets of information: the instructions for use with a conventional oven, and instructions for use with the Omnia.

EQUIPMENT AND UTENSILS

I'm sure you have a pretty good idea of the set-up I have in my little van kitchen. For a bit more clarity, here's a list of everything that I can't do without. Of course, cooking is also possible in a camper van with much less. It really depends on the individual. Personally, I believe a well-equipped kitchen is very important.

APPLIANCES

Omnia (stovetop oven)
Blender/food processor (or stick blender)

Refrigerator with freezer compartment
Milk frother
Kitchen scales

TABLEWARE

2 flat plates
2 shallow bowls
2 large bowls
2 cereal bowls
2 glasses
I salad bowl
Four cutlery sets

KITCHEN UTENSILS

Whisk
Grater
2 saucepans or pots (small and large)
I frying pan
Coffee maker (cafetière)
Coffee grinder
Vegetable peeler
Potholder
Washing-up sponge
Washing-up brush
Tea towel
Chopping board (large and small)
Kitchen knives (large and small)
Wooden spoon
Measuring spoons and cups

STORAGE

Airtight storage containers
Glass jars with screw-top lids
Waxed food storage cloths
Small boxes
Clothes pegs
Cotton bag

Completely plant-based

TIPS FOR A VEGAN DIET

A balanced diet without animal products is neither complicated nor more expensive. There's no need to sacrifice on taste either. Quite the opposite, in fact: A diet of plant-based foods can be incredibly varied, exciting and healthy. And we're also doing something good for the environment, by the way. You'll find out how good plant-based cooking tastes when you try out the dishes included in the recipe section of this book.

Although I've been a vegan for over six years, it's important for me to point out that not everybody wants or is able to eat a purely plant-based diet. Nutrition is a very personal subject and depends on the individual. However, I'm convinced that it is important for us to be aware of the purchasing decision we make, and that we should all take a closer look at what we put on our plates every day. For us and our climate.

Because talk of a vegan diet still gives rise to a great deal of uncertainty and preconceptions, the aim of this chapter is to explain how to create a balanced plant-based meal that gives you all the important nutrients and vitamins without a lot of effort and theory.

My intention is to cater to your current needs: you may want to eat less meat and dairy products, or none at all; or you bought this book just because you want more variety and colour in your diet and would like to have a vegan food day every so often. Whatever your motivation, feel free to find inspiration where you want it and take away what you think you can put to use. This book is an invitation; you decide how far you want to go and at what pace.

HOW DO I 'CONSTRUCT' A BALANCED MEAL FOR MYSELF?

Many of us grew up with meals being planned around meat. So, it comes as no surprise that it can be challenging at first to find the centre of attraction suddenly missing from your plate. All it takes is a little practice to devise a vegan dish that is delicious and filling, while providing you with all the important nutrients.

Personally, I've found that my diet has become much more colourful and varied by taking out animal products. In fact, I've simply become more creative when it comes the need for any more time or additional ingredients. With time and practice, you'll soon get a feel for how to add a new finishing touch to your favourite dishes every time.

The following is a list of great tips and tricks that can add more sophistication and flavour to your meals without much extra effort:

- Add freshly chopped herbs to salads or sprinkle over stews
- Roast nuts and/or seeds, fill a jar and use as a topping for savoury dishes
- Enhance the flavour of dishes at the table with chilli or garlic oil
- Squeeze lemons or limes and drizzle the juice over your dishes
- Make your own seasoned salt blends
- Use nut butter as a topping for sweet breakfast dishes
- Add a dollop of soya yoghurt to savoury dishes
- Combine different flavours: sweet, salty, tangy, bitter and sour flavours often complement each other surprisingly well
- Dare to be creative: the proof of the pudding is in the eating!

INGREDIENT	PROTEIN PER 100 G	DISHES
Tofu	35 g	curries, stir-fried tofu, salads, muesli
Tempeh	35 g	burgers, wraps, Buddha bowls
Chickpeas	25 g	hummus, salads, stews
Lentils	25 g	soups, dhal dishes, moussaka
Beans	25 g	stews, curries, casseroles
Seitan (wheat gluten)	75 g	burgers, Stroganoff, sandwiches
Nuts	18 g	granola (snack), nut butter
Seeds	30 g	muesli, porridge, pasta, curries, granola, protein (bliss) balls, energy bars

HEALTHY COOKING MADE EASY

Our everyday life is often hectic, with little time to actively think about our diet. While I am convinced that we should also prioritise eating well, I'm aware that we have little time for it. That's why it can help to gradually create new routines that allow you to eat in a healthier and more balanced way. You have to start small and, above all, not take on too much right away. There's no point in putting too much pressure on yourself.

INCLUDE FRESH FRUITS AND VEGETABLES AS SNACKS

On days when I know I won't be able to cook much, I like to incorporate healthy and fresh snacks. This also works well when on the road. To do this, I like to chop up a few raw vegetables (carrots, cucumber or tomatoes, for example) and keep them in an airtight container. These keep you fuller for longer if you have them with hummus or another dip. If you prefer sweet snacks, you can also have dried fruits and nuts, or dip apple pieces in a nut butter.

JAZZ UP YOUR BREAKFAST

We often eat the same thing every morning. Jazzing up our breakfast is the ideal way to boost the amount of vitamins and other nutrients. Here are a few ideas:

- Add a little courgette to bircher muesli or porridge.
- If you like muesli with plant-based milk, you could add a spoonful of ground linseed to add more healthy fats, or bake your own crunchy granola at the weekend (three versions are included in the recipe section).
- For people who like to eat bread in the morning, you can spread nut butter on sandwich bread or have sprouts with a country-style loaf. Both provide you with important proteins and keep you full longer than jam or cheese would.

COOKING AHEAD AND STORING IN THE FRIDGE

Do you like eating foods like lentils, brown rice and the like, but they just take too long to prepare of an evening? A good tip is to cook your favourite accompaniments at the beginning of the week and then store them in the fridge. This makes life a lot easier for you on busy days and preparing a balanced meal is much quicker because you only have to cook things to go with them. The same goes for hummus, dips and sauces, for instance. If they are already prepared and waiting in the fridge, you're less likely to reach for shop-bought products or convenience food.

NOT EVERY MEAL HAS TO BE BALANCED

A healthy and balanced diet is one that is varied over time. It's important not to feel bad if you don't prepare any fresh food at all on a given day. What matters is what the food you eat looks like over a week, a month and years. So my first tip is to take the pressure off yourself and don't take everything so seriously. You'll learn that a balanced diet doesn't have to be perfect.

JAZZING UP A TAKEAWAY

I confess that even though I'm passionate about cooking, I actually enjoy not always having to cook. Now that we live in the van, we don't order takeaway very often, but I remember that when we lived in our flat and had it, I would always feel that something was missing. I would chop up a few fresh herbs and add them to the dish, or dice some smoked tofu and mix it into a curry. These and other similar tricks can also give takeaway dishes more freshness and add nutrients.

COOK DOUBLE THE AMOUNT

Most of the recipes in this book are enough for two servings. Of course, if you have enough space in the freezer, you can simply cook double the amount and have a meal ready for another day when time is short.

RECIPES THAT TAKE LESS THAN THIRTY MINUTES TO MAKE

Because I know how much we need to have recipes that can be made and served very quickly, there's a whole chapter in this book with cooking ideas that take less than thirty minutes (page 71).

MY STORE-CUPBOARD ESSENTIALS AND SHOPPING LIST

Even in a camper van, it's practical to always have a basic supply of food on board because any plans we might make can change very quickly. If there is one thing I've learnt, it's that van life is nothing if not unpredictable. Most of the time we start the day without knowing where we'll be sleeping that night. That's why it is always advisable to be prepared. I mean, is there anything worse than going to bed hungry? Right.

By the way, this list is not very different from the one I would have made when I lived in my flat. I guess the only difference is that I don't always have everything within easy reach. Rather, I like to keep three to four different staples handy at all times and then swap them round as soon as the first packet is finished. This list is meant to be more of an inspiration for you, and it may also contain some foods that are no longer so easy to find, such as heritage grains, which I'm doing my part to revive with some of the recipes in my book. But see for yourself:

FOR THE STORE-CUPBOARD

Sunflower seeds

Walnuts

Hazelnuts

Linseed

Hemp seed

Balsamic vinegar

Apple concentrate

Rice syrup

Garlic

Onions

Rapeseed oil

Olive oil

Nut butter

PASTA, CEREALS AND PULSES

Rolled oats
Pearl barley
Risotto rice
Brown rice
Basmati rice
Millet
Couscous
Whole brown lentils
Red and green lentils
Wholemeal pasta
Spaghetti
Potatoes
Buckwheat
Chickpeas
Haricot beans
Cornmeal

SPICES

Salt
Black pepper
Dried Mediterranean herb mix
Cardamom
Ground cloves
Coriander
Smoked paprika
Cinnamon
Nutmeg
Yeast flakes
Garlic powder
Turmeric powder
Vegetable stock powder

FLOURS

Light spelt flour
Wholemeal flour
Soya flour
Oat flour
Baking powder

IN THE FRIDGE

Mustard
Sambal oelek
Ginger
Seasonal vegetables
Seasonal fruits
Oat or soya cream
Oat milk
Soya yoghurt
Fresh herbs
Lemons
Tomato purée

IN THE FREEZER

Berries
Herbs
Leaf vegetables
Bananas
Chestnuts

SUSTAINABILITY AND ENVIRONMENTAL AWARENESS ON THE GO

For me, living an environmentally aware and healthy life doesn't stop at nutrition. Therefore, this chapter explores how we can travel in the most resource-efficient and environmentally friendly way possible, and the things to which we've actively been paying attention since moving into the van.

A GUEST IN NATURE

Travelling in a camper van also means living with and in nature. It's important for us to always remind ourselves that we are only guests at camping and caravan sites. Free camping is an absolute honour. And to make this at all possible, it's up to all van livers to abide by certain unwritten rules. So, we have drawn up our own little code of conduct.

We leave pitches cleaner than how we found them. Having a supply of rubber gloves and refuse sacks on the van is a must. We use them to pick up the rubbish previous guests leave.

Free camping — also known as wild camping — is a legal grey area in many countries. It's important to us not to disturb anyone, which is why we don't spend the night in inhabited areas; we don't make noise, and we stow away our tables and chairs in the van overnight. Besides, we never stay at the one camping or caravan site for days or weeks at a time.

The big problem with free camping is that it benefits the local economy very little. We try to give something back by shopping at small local establishments, visiting farmers' markets and having coffee out, and also by regularly staying at camping and caravan sites.

Nature isn't a toilet, which is why we opted for a compact dry separation toilet on the van. It takes up very little space and is super easy to clean; it's also much more environmentally friendly than a chemical toilet.

BETTER THAN SHOP-BOUGHT

Many products that were once commonly made in every home are now easily available in every supermarket. This is a great thing on the one hand because, given our hectic lives, we can't always make time to cook or bake everything ourselves. But on the other hand, I also find it nice to consciously take time to bake bread or make my own spice mixes.

So, this chapter contains my favourite recipes for basics that can be whipped up in no time. For instance, they include three varieties of granola you toast in a frying pan and which taste much better than store-bought ever could. There are also very special treats that I prefer to make in my own kitchen rather than buy, whenever possible. These include my moist and nutritious carrot and quark bread, and my seed blend, a nutty-flavoured topping that turns any pasta dish, no matter how simple, into a crowd-pleaser. I've also come up with recipes for a tofu ricotta and a vegan feta cheese that you can't buy anywhere.

Tofu ricotta

It's almost outrageous how simple this recipe is and how delicious the result. Once you've tried it, you'll need to keep a constant supply of it in the fridge.

MAKES APPROX. 300 G

250 g tofu

50 ml soya milk

2 tbsp lemon juice

2 tbsp olive oil

I pinch salt

¼ tsp garlic powder

2 tbsp yeast flakes

½ bunch basil, chopped

Use a blender or food processor, or a stick blender to blend all the ingredients, except the basil, until creamy but still slightly crumbly. Finally, fold in the freshly chopped basil. Press the mixture into a cheese mould and leave to drain in the fridge for several hours or overnight. Alternatively, use immediately.

Marinated vegan feta cheese

Whether as an hors d'oeuvre served with grissini breadsticks and olives, or as a topping for savoury dishes, this feta cheese made from marinated tofu is so tangy that even people who don't like tofu will enjoy it.

MAKES 250 ML (1 JAR)

200 g regular tofu

6 tbsp olive oil

1 tbsp yeast flakes

1 tsp dried Mediterranean herb mix

½ tsp garlic powder

Salt and pepper

Drain the tofu, wrap in a clean cloth and squeeze, then cut into small cubes.

Make a marinade by mixing the remaining ingredients and coat the tofu well. Put everything into a jar, shake well and marinate overnight in the refrigerator. The tofu feta will keep for at least two weeks.

Carrot and quark bread

This recipe requires no flour or heavy kneading. Not only is this high-fibre bread, made with oat flakes, carrots and pumpkin seeds, impressive for its nutritional value but also for its rich flavour. It goes perfectly with both sweet and savoury spreads.

MAKES I LOAF (LOAF TIN UP TO 25 CM LONG)

100 g carrots

300 g pinhead oatmeal

100 g soya yoghurt

100 g pumpkin seeds

2 tsp salt

2 tbsp linseed, coarsely ground

200 ml cold water

Oil, for greasing

Peel and grate the carrots. Mix in a bowl with the remaining ingredients and use clean, cold hands to knead well until incorporated. Put the mixture into a greased loaf tin and press to compact. Brush with a little water and bake in a convection oven at 180°C for 65 minutes. If using an Omnia, this takes about the same amount of time on a medium heat.

This bread stays fresh and moist for several days, even lasting up to a week if kept in the fridge. It can also be frozen.

Herb salt

When we were in Greece, we would often pick fresh herbs, dry them and then make them into a herb salt. This is a wonderful way to make use of the last herbs growing on the balcony before winter. It also makes the perfect gift.

MAKES 250 ML (1 JAR)

10 sprigs thyme

5 sprigs rosemary

3 tbsp olive oil

200 g coarse salt

Zest of ½ lemon, grated

Finely chop the thyme and rosemary. Sauté in a frying pan with the olive oil, then add the salt. After 2 minutes, add the lemon zest and turn off the heat. Fill a jar with the herb salt.

Red curry paste

It isn't easy to find a good Thai curry paste made without fish sauce. That's why I like to make my own, which I freeze so that I always have some handy.

MAKES 200 ML (1 JAR)

12 red chilli peppers, dried

4 red onions

8 cloves garlic

1 ½ tbsp fresh ginger, chopped

2 stalks lemongrass

1 tsp cumin seeds

½ tsp ground cinnamon

¼ tsp ground cloves

3 tbsp sesame oil (or coconut oil)

Pour boiling water over the chillies and leave to soak. After 15 minutes, split them open and remove the seeds. Chop the onions and garlic and sauté in a frying pan with the oil and other ingredients, stirring constantly. Add the contents to the chillies in a blender or food processor and purée until the lemongrass is finely chopped. Transfer the paste to a clean jar, cover with a little oil and store in the fridge. It will keep for about four weeks in the fridge. I also like to divide the paste into portions and freeze them. An ice tray works best for this.

My seed blend

This vegan grated cheese substitute enhances practically any dish while adding an extra hint of spice.

MAKES 250 ML (1 JAR)

100 g roasted sunflower seeds

50 g toasted pine nuts

5 tbsp yeast flakes

1 tsp garlic powder

½ tsp sweet paprika

2 tbsp olive oil

Salt and pepper

Toast the sunflower seeds and pine nuts briefly in a frying pan and grind to a powder in a bender or food processor. Combine them in a bowl with the remaining ingredients and mix well. Store in an airtight jar in the fridge. The mixture will keep for a fortnight.

Pumpkin spice

Pumpkin spice is a spice mix that is particularly popular in the United States. But it's very easy to make yourself. I like to use it on my breakfast and when baking, such as in cakes and muffins.

MAKES 100 ML (1 SMALL JAR)

10 tsp ground cinnamon

5 tsp ground ginger

2 tsp ground cloves

1 tsp freshly grated nutmeg

1 pinch vanilla powder

1 pinch salt

Thoroughly mix all the ingredients in a small bowl. Optionally, you can also add sugar. The mixture will keep for a few months in an airtight container.

Summer focaccia

It isn't summer without focaccia. My family used to go to Tuscany, in Italy, every July. And whenever we went, focaccia would be served at every opportunity, either home-made or shop-bought. This recipe works particularly well however you want to use it. This light and airy bread tastes best when still a little warm. A really good organic olive oil is essential for any focaccia recipe.

MAKES 6

320 g light spelt flour

1 ½ tsp sugar

1 tsp salt

½ cube (21 g) fresh yeast

160 ml lukewarm water

Olive oil

½ red onion

1 handful olives

1 handful baby plum tomatoes

3 sprigs thyme

2 pinches sea salt

Oil, for greasing

Mix the flour with the sugar and salt in a bowl. Dissolve the yeast in the lukewarm water and add to the bowl, together with 4 tablespoons of olive oil. Mix with your hands to form a dough, then knead until smooth. Cover the dough with a damp cloth and leave to rise in a warm place for at least 30 minutes. Place the dough directly on a greased baking tray lined with baking parchment. Spread it over the tray and press flat to a thickness of 2–3 cm. Rest the dough for 15 more minutes.

In the meantime, slice the onion into rings, pit the olives, halve the tomatoes and pluck the thyme. Brush the focaccia with olive oil and spread the toppings over it. Sprinkle with a little sea salt and bake in a preheated oven at 220°C, top and bottom heat, for about 25 minutes. If using an Omnia, bake the focaccia in a greased silicone liner for about 30 minutes on a high heat.

FOR CREATIVE MINDS

Instead of scattering the tomatoes and olives randomly on the focaccia, you can create an attractive pattern or even a meadow of flowers. For the latter, you can use peppers of different colours or fresh herbs. There are no limits to your creativity in this respect. If you prefer to score points for flavour rather than appearance, you can drizzle a little truffle olive oil over the focaccia immediately after baking. Heavenly!

Toasted granola with lemon and tahini

You can now buy granola at any supermarket, but nothing tastes as good as the crispy granola you can make yourself. It's also healthier. The beauty of this recipe is that you don't need to use the oven.

MAKES 500 ML (I LARGE JAR WITH SCREW-TOP LID)

300 g nuts of your choice
(hazelnuts, walnuts, almonds)

150 g dried figs

4 tbsp rapeseed oil

350 g pinhead oatmeal

2 tbsp tahini

Zest of I lemon

7 tbsp pear concentrate
(or other liquid sweetener)

I pinch salt

Chop up the nuts and figs and sauté in a frying pan with the rapeseed oil. Gradually add the remaining ingredients and toast in the pan, stirring constantly, until the granola turns golden brown.

Leave everything to cool down completely, then fill an airtight screw-top jar. This crispy granola tastes great with fresh fruit and vegan yoghurt or oat milk. It will stay fresh for a good two weeks.

A GREAT GIFT IDEA

You can never go wrong with an extra jar of granola on the pantry shelf or in the kitchen cupboard. Actually, I sometimes make a gift of it to people we meet along the way. Eyes light up to find such a pretty jar of home-made granola. It can also be a nice gift idea for birthdays and special occasions.

Crispy chocolate granola

This recipe is dedicated to Chris. I affectionately call him my chocolate tiger, because he devours anything chocolatey in a flash. So, if you share his love for chocolate, you'd be better off making double the amount. It can be quite addictive.

MAKES 500 ML (1 LARGE JAR WITH SCREW-TOP LID)

150 g cashew nuts

150 g coarse rolled oats

15 g puffed millet (or quinoa)

25 ml rapeseed oil

40 ml rice syrup

1 pinch salt

4 tbsp cocoa powder

1 tsp ground cinnamon

45 g currants (or raisins)

20 g cocoa nibs

20 g hemp seeds

Chop and toast the cashews in a dry frying pan. Add all the remaining ingredients — except the currants, cocoa nibs and hemp seeds — and toast everything on a low heat, stirring constantly, until crispy. After about 12 minutes, remove from the heat and sprinkle in the remaining ingredients. Leave the granola to cool in the pan and then fill a jar. The granola will keep for a good three weeks.

Quick nut granola

This crispy granola can be prepared in 10 minutes, filling your kitchen with the sweet smell of cinnamon and orange. It tastes best with plant-based milk or soya yoghurt.

MAKES 500 ML (1 LARGE JAR)

100 g hazelnuts

80 g shelled pistachio nuts

250 g oats

10 tbsp rapeseed oil

6 tbsp rice syrup

1 tsp ground cinnamon

1 pinch salt

Zest of ½ orange

Chop and toast the nuts in a non-stick pan. Add the remaining ingredients and allow the granola to caramelise while stirring constantly. Turn off the heat after 10 minutes and leave to cool in the pan. Fill a jar and store inside an airtight container. The granola will stay fresh for a fortnight.

BREAKFAST

I'm the kind of person who can have the same thing for breakfast every day. And that's often the case, to be honest. Actually, my favourite way to start the day is with a hot breakfast, which typically means porridge. That's also why there are three different porridge recipes in this chapter.

But I'm also a big fan of brunch at the weekend. Besides creamy smoothie bowls and fluffy pancakes, I'll also serve hearty dishes such as a shakshuka and vegan egg sandwiches.

Blueberry and poppy seed pancake

Summer in Sweden is wild blueberry season. Every time we would go for a walk or hike, we could pick the wild berries. They're bursting with vitamins and antioxidants, and are much more aromatic than the blueberries you find in supermarkets. Wild blueberries can also be found in many other countries in Europe and all over the United States. They are especially delicious in pancakes.

SERVES 2

For the linseed egg
I tsp linseed

For the pancakes
I linseed egg (see above)
200 g light spelt flour
2 tsp baking powder
I pinch salt
I tbsp poppy seeds
Zest of ½ lemon
2 tbsp sugar
300 ml oat milk
I handful blueberries
4 tbsp rapeseed oil

For the linseed egg, grind I teaspoon of linseed to a powder and mix with 4 tablespoons of water. Leave to hydrate for 10 minutes.

For the batter, mix all the dry ingredients with the linseed egg and oat milk. Fold in the berries only at the end. Heat the rapeseed oil in a frying pan and fry the pancakes on both sides, flipping after 30 seconds. Serve the pancakes with granola, extra berries and a little apple concentrate, or another sweetener.

FREEZE BERRIES IN SUMMER
It makes good sense to pick berries at the height of the season and freeze them in an airtight container for the colder months. They retain both their vitamins and flavour.

Tiramisu smoothie bowl

Even though tiramisu is a dessert, I love it so much that I could eat it every morning. Here is a healthier breakfast option that I can guarantee to be just as delicious!

SERVES 2

For the smoothie
1 ½ bananas
4 pitted dates
400 g silken tofu
1 ½ tbsp cocoa powder
10 coffee beans
1 pinch salt

For the cream
150 g natural soya yoghurt, unsweetened
Zest of ¼ lemon
1 ½ tsp sugar
Chocolate granola (see recipe on page 41) for decoration

Blend all the ingredients together, including the salt, in a blender or food processor to make a smoothie, then divide into two bowls. In a separate bowl, mix the soya yoghurt with the lemon zest and sugar and spread the cream over the smoothie. Serve with chocolate granola.

Shakshuka

Shakshuka is a speciality of North African and Israeli cuisines that is typically made with poached eggs, tomatoes and onions. This dish tastes good at any time of the day. We love it for our weekend brunch. It's packed with good proteins and has a really delicious, spicy taste.

SERVES 2–3

1 onion
3 cloves garlic
2 tbsp olive oil
2 red peppers
250 g tofu
400 g baby plum tomatoes
1 tsp balsamic vinegar glaze
1 tsp smoked paprika
1 tsp ground coriander
½ tsp ground caraway
1 tsp sesame seeds
½ tsp ground cinnamon
300 ml tomato passata
   (sieved tomatoes)
Salt and pepper
250 g cooked haricot beans
1 tbsp tahini
Juice of ½ lemon
½ tsp salt
½ tsp garlic powder

Chop the onion and garlic and sauté in a frying pan with the olive oil. Remove the seeds from the peppers and slice into thin strips. Drain and squeeze the tofu, then cut into cubes. Add the peppers and tofu to the pan and sauté. Halve and add the tomatoes. Season with the balsamic vinegar glaze and all the spices. Stir in the passata, lower the heat and leave everything to cook down. Season with salt and pepper.

Use a blender or food processor, or a stick blender to purée the beans with the remaining ingredients until creamy, then add a few dollops to the pan. Simmer for a few minutes without stirring, then serve hot in the pan. It goes well with pita or regular bread.

Spiced porridge

After a chilly night in the van, my morning porridge is like a warm embrace. The warming spices are particularly good for the stomach. Hot porridge is just about the healthiest thing you can eat in the morning.

SERVES 2

2 ripe bananas

120 g oats of your choice

½ tsp ground cinnamon

½ tsp pumpkin spice
  (see recipe on page 34)

1 pinch salt

350 ml oat milk

Water, as needed

Mash the bananas with a fork and combine in a saucepan with all the dry ingredients. Add half the oat milk and cook the porridge on a medium heat, stirring constantly. Gradually add the rest of the oat milk, diluting with a little water if the porridge becomes too thick. Serve warm with fresh fruit, nut butter and granola.

MAKE YOUR OWN GRANOLA
You can buy granola anywhere, but it's much better and more nutritious to make yourself. This book contains three granola recipes (pages 38, 41 and 42). There's a little something for everyone.

Muesli with stewed plums

This recipe is for people who aren't fans of porridge but still want to incorporate more oats into their diet. The combination of cold muesli and warm stewed plums makes this breakfast so delicious.

SERVES 2

For the muesli
100 g oats
100 ml lukewarm water
300 g soya yoghurt
I tsp psyllium husk powder
2 tsp apple concentrate
I tsp ground cinnamon
2 pinches ground cardamom

For the stewed plums
8 plums
I tsp rapeseed oil
I tsp apple concentrate
½ tsp ground cinnamon

Grind the oats into a powder in a blender or food processor and mix with the remaining muesli ingredients to form a paste. Divide into two bowls.

De-stone and quarter the plums. Heat the oil in a saucepan and sauté the plums with the apple concentrate and cinnamon until soft and slightly caramelised. Arrange the stewed plums over the muesli and enjoy lukewarm. This muesli goes well with granola and nut butter.

'Egg' mayonnaise open sandwiches

Especially at weekends, we love nothing more than a nice morning run followed by brunch. It's typically a hearty meal. These open sandwiches can be made in no time at all and taste absolutely delicious. They're the perfect pick-me-up after a sweaty workout.

MAKES 4

150 g regular tofu

150 g silken tofu

1 handful fresh chives

2 tsp vegan mayonnaise

1 tsp mustard

Juice of ¼ lemon

½ tsp turmeric powder

1 tsp yeast flakes

¼ tsp kala namak (Himalayan black salt)

¼ tsp salt

4 slices of the bread of your choice

Roasted sunflower seeds

Pepper

Using clean fingers, crumble the tofu into a bowl. Add the silken tofu. Then finely chop the chives and lightly stir in together with all the remaining ingredients. Mix well with a fork to achieve the consistency of real egg mayonnaise. Spread the mixture on the bread and serve garnished with some roasted sunflower seeds and seasoned with freshly ground pepper.

SILKEN TOFU SUBSTITUTE
Silken tofu isn't always available everywhere. The 'egg' mayonnaise will turn out just as good if you only use regular tofu. In this case, simply mix in a dash of a plant-based milk until you achieve the desired consistency.

Chestnut smoothie with salted caramel sauce

Chestnut season is far too short; I'm sure you'll agree. Personally, I love sinking my teeth into anything with chestnuts, even first thing in the morning.

For the smoothie

2 frozen bananas

200 g chestnuts, peeled and boiled

400 g silken tofu

½ tsp ground cinnamon

½-cm length fresh ginger

I pinch ground cardamom

For the caramel sauce

6 soft pitted dates

I dash oat milk

2 tsp blanched almond butter

¼ tsp cocoa powder

2 pinches salt

Granola, for garnishing

For the smoothie, blend all the ingredients in a blender or food processor until smooth and creamy. Divide into two bowls. Then purée the dates with the oat milk, almond butter, cocoa powder and salt. Drizzle the caramel sauce over the smoothie. Garnish with granola and serve.

Stewed apple porridge

It's no secret that I love porridge. However, this recipe is my favourite by far. I could eat porridge like this every day. Well, at least after a relatively cool night.

SERVES 2

For the porridge

120 g oats of your choice

350 ml oat milk

1 ½ tbsp apple concentrate
(or other liquid sweetener)

½ tsp ground cinnamon

1 pinch salt

For the stewed apple

2 small tart apples

1 tbsp rapeseed oil

3 tbsp apple purée

1 handful raisins

1 tsp ground cinnamon

2 tsp apple concentrate
(or other liquid sweetener)

In a saucepan, bring the oats to the boil with the remaining porridge ingredients on a medium heat while stirring constantly. Then turn off the heat, cover with a lid and leave to stand.

In the meantime, core, finely dice and sauté the apples in a second saucepan with the remaining ingredients until soft.

Briefly reheat the porridge to the desired consistency and divide into two bowls. Spread the stewed apple over the porridge and serve hot. It can be enjoyed with mulberries (or other dried berries), nut butter or other toppings of your choice.

WHY PORRIDGE IS SO HEALTHY
Cooked oats have a positive effect on our intestinal flora while providing us with important B-group vitamins, magnesium, calcium and iron. They also keep you full for a long time because they're high in fibre.

Blueberry smoothie bowl

This smoothie bowl makes the perfect snack for between meals and for people who don't like a big breakfast. Very few ingredients are required. You can also make it when blueberries are in season and freeze it to enjoy in the winter months.

MAKES 2 SMALL PORTIONS

300 g frozen blueberries

200 g soya yoghurt

1 handful fresh spinach

2 ½ tbsp apple concentrate

Juice and zest of ½ lemon

1 pinch ground cinnamon

Blend all the ingredients in a blender or food processor and serve with granola, fruit, hemp seeds and nut butter.

SILKEN TOFU INSTEAD OF SOYA YOGHURT
Silken tofu can also be used as an alternative for the soya yoghurt. This will makes the result even lighter and fluffier, and it can also be enjoyed as a healthy dessert.

Summer bircher muesli

For a taste of home while on the road, we like to have bircher muesli for breakfast from time to time. The variation shown here is one of my favourites. The hint of lemon makes it particularly refreshing and summery.

SERVES 2

400 g soya yoghurt

80 g oats

1 apple, cored and grated

30 g chopped walnuts

Zest and juice of ½ lemon

4 tsp linseed, coarsely ground

3 tsp hemp seeds

3 tsp apple concentrate
  (or other sweetener)

3 tsp almond butter

30 g raisins

½ tsp ground cinnamon

2 tsp nut butter of your choice

Mix all the ingredients, except the nut butter, in a bowl and leave to soak for 20 minutes. Serve with the nut butter, as well as granola and fresh fruit.

FOR THAT EXTRA VITAMIN BOOST
If you find it difficult to eat enough vegetables throughout the day, you can also grate a small courgette into your muesli. It won't affect the flavour.

Spiced carrot porridge

Carrots for breakfast? Why not? This porridge tastes like a delicious cake batter and reminds me a little of Christmas.

SERVES 2

2 carrots

½-cm length fresh ginger

100 g rolled oats

1 tsp ground cinnamon

2 pinches ground cardamom

1 pinch ground cloves

30 g raisins

2 tsp apple concentrate

1 apple, cored and grated

120 ml water

400 ml oat milk

2 tsp linseed

1 pinch salt

Finely grate the carrots and ginger. Combine in a saucepan with the rest of the dry ingredients, apple concentrate and grated apple. Add half of both the water and the oat milk and place on a medium heat. Stir constantly as the oats cook, gradually adding water and oat milk until the porridge has a creamy consistency.

Then turn off the heat, cover with a lid and leave to stand for 5 more minutes. This time will allow the spices to properly infuse the porridge.

Divide the porridge into two bowls and enjoy warm with chopped pistachios, nut butter and a little soya yoghurt.

French toast with peach

This recipe was born out of necessity. We were in the middle of nowhere with little food left, and very hungry. It wasn't originally my intention to include this dish in the book, but it was so delicious that we've been having French toast for breakfast ever since, especially whenever our bread goes too stale to enjoy.

SERVES 2

5–6 slices stale bread

I banana

180 ml plant-based milk

I tsp maple syrup

I pinch ground cinnamon

I pinch salt

2 peaches, quartered

3 tbsp rapeseed oil

Blend all the ingredients, except the sliced bread, peaches and oil, in a blender or food processor, or with a stick blender until smooth. Then soak the bread slices in the mixture until fully saturated. In a frying pan with oil, fry each slice of bread on both sides until golden brown. Then set the French toast aside and briefly sauté the peaches in the same frying pan until they become fragrant.

Stack the French toast on a plate and top with the peaches. Enjoy this breakfast with date syrup and granola.

FOR LOVERS OF A HEARTY BREAKFAST
While French toast is typically a sweet dish, they can just as easily come in a savoury version. Instead of banana, I make the soaking mixture by combining soya or chickpea flour with a little water, oil, salt and spices, and then I use whatever I like as a topping.

HEARTY MEALS IN LESS THAN THIRTY MINUTES

This chapter is dedicated to everybody who likes to eat well but often can't afford to spend long hours in the kitchen. I promise you that all these dishes will be ready to enjoy on your table in thirty minutes or under. Healthy and delicious food doesn't have to be time-consuming or complicated.

By the way, the quick peanut curry is a big hit with us. We cook it at least once a week because it tastes so good and is so quick to make at the same time. Also highly recommended is the cacio e pepe, a pasta dish that goes down a treat after a long and hard day.

Watermelon and cucumber salad

Watermelons could be bought on every corner in Greece. Admittedly, we ate most of our fruit plain. But we also quite often chopped up watermelon to make this refreshing salad. It's particularly great for hot summer days when cooking is out of the question.

For a special occasion recipe can be found on page 30.

SERVES 2

For the salad

½ baby watermelon

1 cucumber

1 tomato

1 red onion

3 sprigs dill

For the dressing

1-cm length fresh ginger

1 clove garlic

1 tbsp peanut butter

3 tbsp soy sauce

3 tbsp balsamic vinegar

1 tsp pear concentrate
  (or other sweetener)

Juice of ½ lemon

Pepper

Black sesame seeds, for
  garnishing

Peel and dice the watermelon. Cut the cucumber and tomato into bite-sized pieces and the onion into thin strips. Pluck the dill and combine everything in a bowl.

For the dressing, blend all the ingredients, except the pepper and sesame seeds, in a blender or food processor, or with a stick blender until smooth. Pour the dressing into the salad and toss well. Season with freshly ground pepper, garnish with black sesame seeds and serve. If desired, vegan feta cheese can be crumbled and gently mixed in as well. For a striking effect, use a vegetable peeler to shave a few cucumber ribbons and roll them up.

FOR A SPECIAL OCCASION
This refreshing salad goes incredibly well with a vegan feta cheese you can marinate at home. It definitely adds a special touch. The recipe can be found on page 30.

Quick peanut curry with tofu

As the name suggests, this dish will be steaming hot and ready to enjoy in no time at all. It's ideal for curry-lovers who don't want to spend a lot of time in the kitchen but still like to eat healthy, balanced and delicious food.

SERVES 2

1 cup basmati rice

2 cups water

2 cloves garlic

1 red onion

2 tbsp rapeseed oil

150 g regular tofu

2 tbsp soy sauce

1 aubergine, cut into small pieces

1 red pepper, cut into small pieces

½ head broccoli, cut into small pieces

For the sauce

1 tsp smoked paprika

¼ tsp chilli powder

250 ml oat or soya cream

1 tbsp peanut butter

1 ½-cm length fresh ginger

2 tsp pear concentrate (or other sweetener)

2 tbsp soy sauce

Cook the rice in the water according to the instructions on the packet. Chop the garlic and onion and sauté in a large frying pan with the rapeseed oil.

Cut the tofu into bite-sized pieces and sauté as well. When golden, deglaze the pan with the soy sauce and add the remaining vegetables. Sauté for 10 minutes more, stirring constantly.

Use a blender or food processor, or a stick blender to purée the sauce ingredients and add to the vegetables. Lower the heat and simmer for 5 minutes, until the sauce thickens.

Fill a cup with cooked rice and press firmly to compact. Turn the rice out on a plate and serve with the curry. Freshly chopped herbs, such as mint, parsley or coriander, and chopped peanuts are suitable toppings. Season with a dash of lemon juice if desired.

MARINATE TOFU FOR DELICIOUS FLAVOUR

People who find tofu boring often haven't found the right marinade for it yet. Tofu is actually rather tasteless, but with the right seasoning it becomes a really tasty source of protein. So, if you remember to marinate the tofu the night before, this curry will make you even happier. My four favourite tofu marinades can be found on page 178.

Cacio e pepe

This pasta dish is a speciality of Rome, which is where I first tried it. The sauce is traditionally made with lots of cheese and cream. In my version, the creaminess and seasoning is provided by the beans and yeast flakes.

SERVES 2

300 g pasta of your choice

300 g cooked cannellini (or haricot) beans

20 g cashew butter

2 tbsp olive oil

40 ml soya cream

4 tbsp yeast flakes

I tsp garlic powder

Salt and pepper

Cook the pasta according to the instructions on the packet. In the meantime, use a blender or food processor, or a stick blender to blend the remaining ingredients into a creamy sauce. When al dente, drain the pasta, setting aside some of the cooking water. Mix the pasta with the sauce, stirring in some of the cooking water if necessary, and serve immediately.

Home-made seed blend makes a good topping for a more intense cheesy flavour (see recipe on page 34).

Poke bowl with crispy tofu and peanut sauce

I love dishes that can always be reinvented and varied, which is why I'm a big fan of the poke bowl. Originally from Hawaii, it traditionally contains raw fish, vegetables, rice and dressing. My version replaces the fish with tofu.

SERVES 2

250 g tofu

Juice of 1 lemon

2 tbsp peanut butter

2 tbsp sesame oil

1 ½–2-cm length fresh ginger

1 tsp apple concentrate
  (or other sweetener)

5 tbsp tamari (or conventional
  soy sauce)

50 ml coconut milk

1 clove garlic

1 cup jasmine rice or other
  long-grain rice variety

2 cups water

1 cucumber

1 carrot

1 handful baby plum tomatoes

Fresh mint, chopped

Toasted sesame seeds

Cut the tofu into bite-sized pieces. Use a blender or food processor, or a stick blender to blend the lemon juice, peanut butter, sesame oil, ginger, apple concentrate, tamari, coconut milk and garlic to a sauce. Marinate the tofu in a bowl with 5 tablespoons of the sauce.

Set aside the remaining sauce.

Cook the rice in the water according to the instructions on the packet. In the meantime, fry the tofu well on all sides in a non-stick frying pan until golden brown. Use a vegetable peeler to shave the cucumber and carrot lengthwise into thin ribbons. Halve the tomatoes.

Serve everything together in a bowl with some freshly chopped mint and toasted sesame seeds. The rice looks very appealing when compacted inside a smaller bowl and turned out into the bowl. A cup can also be used. Serve the poke bowl lukewarm or cold. Drizzle over with sauce just before serving.

ALREADY PREPARED AND WAITING
Since poke bowls taste great cold, this dish is perfect to prepare the night before and take with you if you are out and about the next day. A great meal that looks as good as it tastes.

Spaghetti with pesto, sweet potato and celeriac

We enjoyed this steaming plate of pasta after a long and strenuous hike in the Norwegian mountains. Although the combination of sweet potato, celery and pear sounds quite bold, it's really incredibly delicious.

SERVES 2

3 cloves garlic

2 onions

2 tbsp olive oil

1 large sweet potato, finely diced

½ celeriac, finely diced

1 pear, diced

6 sage leaves, chopped

1 tsp dried Italian herbs

½ tsp salt

1 dash white wine

50 ml water

200 ml oat cream

3 tsp pesto

250 g wholewheat spaghetti

1 handful sunflower seeds

Fresh parsley or coriander

Juice and zest of ½ lemon

Chop the garlic and onions and sauté in a frying pan with the oil. Then add the diced vegetables and sauté. After 5 minutes, add the pear, sage, herbs and salt. Deglaze the pan with the white wine and add the water. Simmer until the vegetables are soft. Mix in the oat cream and 2 teaspoons of pesto. Lower the heat.

In the meantime, cook the spaghetti according to the instructions on the packet, then pour off the water and leave to drain. Serve the pasta with the sauce in large plates and drizzle over with the remaining pesto. Garnish with sunflower seeds and a few fresh herbs. Finally, drizzle the lemon juice and sprinkle the lemon zest over the spaghetti. Serve hot.

VARYING WITH THE SEASON
Instead of sweet potato, which is often only in season for a short time, you can use a winter squash or carrots to make this dish.

Broccoli and chickpea salad

Broccoli is by far my favourite vegetable. And not only cooked, but also raw in salads. This Mediterranean cabbage variety is even healthier uncooked. Broccoli contains a lot of vitamin C and important minerals.

SERVES 2

½ cucumber

1 tomato

1 red onion

1 handful fresh mint

1 handful fresh coriander

6 lettuce leaves (or other salad leaves)

1 small head broccoli

5 dried figs

250 g cooked chickpeas

For the dressing

4 tsp olive oil

Juice of 1 lime

1 tsp miso paste

1 ½ tbsp soy sauce

2 tsp liquid sweetener

2 tsp tahini

1-cm length fresh ginger

1 clove garlic

1 dash water

1 handful chopped peanuts

Cut the cucumber and tomato into bite-sized pieces. Chop the onion and fresh herbs. Finely chop the lettuce, broccoli and dried figs. Combine everything in a bowl with the cooked chickpeas.

To make the dressing, use a blender or food processor, or a stick blender to blend all the ingredients, except the peanuts, and pour onto the salad. Toss well and allow to infuse briefly, then sprinkle with the chopped peanuts and serve immediately.

EATING BROCCOLI WITHOUT FLATULENCE
Broccoli florets are more easily digested than the stalk. So, if you have a sensitive gut, it's better not to include the stalk. But you don't have to throw it away. Chopped into small pieces, it can be used for any pasta dish or to make soups.

Quick chilli sin carne

Before Chris and I decided to live in our own camper van, we had already been on several van holidays. During our first holiday in Sweden, in particular, we ate this everywhere because the evenings were so cold that we needed something quick to warm us up inside.

SERVES 2

2 cloves garlic

2 onions

3 tbsp olive oil

150 g sunflower mince

1 tsp smoked paprika

½ tsp chilli powder

¼ tsp ground coriander

¼ tsp dried oregano

150 ml vegetable stock

3 tbsp tomato purée

2 tbsp balsamic vinegar glaze

400 g chopped tomatoes

250 g cooked black beans

250 g sweetcorn

Salt and pepper

Freshly chopped parsley

1 tbsp vegan yoghurt

Chop the garlic and onions and sauté in a frying pan with the olive oil. Add the sunflower mince and spices and sauté on a high heat, stirring constantly. Deglaze the pan with the vegetable stock and immediately add the tomato purée and balsamic vinegar glaze. Simmer briefly, then add the remaining ingredients (except salt and pepper, parsley and yoghurt) as well. Season with a little salt and pepper and continue to simmer. The longer the chilli sits on the hob, the better it tastes. Serve with freshly chopped parsley and vegan yoghurt.

Tortilla chips, jalapeños and lime juice also go well.

MORE IDEAS FOR VEGAN CHILLI
Instead of sunflower mince, you can make it with textured vegetable protein or lentils. It can also be served with a side of rice.

Tahini and lemon noodle stir-fry

It's no secret that I love tahini and lemon together. The combination also works wonderfully with noodle dishes. This recipe will come in handy when you're short on time.

SERVES 2

1 clove garlic

2 tbsp sesame oil

1 small aubergine

1 sweet pointed pepper

250 g soba (buckwheat) noodles

2 tbsp tahini

Juice and zest of 1 lemon

80 ml oat cream

Salt and pepper

Chop the garlic and sauté in a frying pan with the sesame oil until golden brown. Cut the aubergine and pepper into bite-sized slivers and sauté in the pan with the garlic.

In the meantime, cook the noodles according to the instructions on the packet, then pour off the water and leave to drain. As soon as the vegetables are golden brown, add the noodles to the pan. Lightly stir in the tahini and the lemon juice and zest. Add the oat cream and season with salt and pepper.

FOR AN EXTRA NUTTY TASTE
Toasted sesame seeds make the perfect topping for this dish. Black sesame seeds look particularly appealing. As we all know, we eat with our eyes.

Chickpea and melon salad

There were weeks in Greece when it was simply too hot to eat anything but cold food. This salad was an absolute lifesaver on such days. The juicy melon makes it nice and fruity, and the chickpeas keep you full for longer.

SERVES 2

½ melon (honeydew or Galia)

I fennel bulb

I red onion

250 g cooked chickpeas

2 oranges

2 tsp mustard

I tsp apple concentrate
  (or other sweetener)

4 tbsp white balsamic vinegar

2 tbsp olive oil

¼ tsp salt

Pepper

I pinch chilli flakes

Cut the melon into bite-sized pieces and the fennel into thin strips and chop the onion.

Set the fennel fronds aside for garnishing. Combine the melon, fennel and onion in a bowl with the chickpeas. Segment one of the oranges and add to the bowl. Squeeze the second orange, mix the juice with the remaining ingredients to make a dressing and pour into the bowl as well. Toss well, then arrange the salad on plates, garnish with the fennel fronds and serve.

FOR MORE BEARABLE DAYS
The salad tastes particularly good if, instead of using it raw, the fennel is quickly sautéed in a hot pan with a little olive oil, salt and pepper.

Pesto and hummus bruschetta

There's nothing like crusty bread topped with sun-ripened tomatoes. Bruschetta is a classic part of Italian cuisine. Personally, however, it tastes even better in combination with a creamy lemon hummus and the light tang of pistachio pesto. It might sound odd, but it's mighty good!

MAKES 5

5 slices white bread

3 tbsp olive oil

2 large tomatoes

I red onion

I tsp balsamic vinegar glaze

¼ tsp salt

2 pinches ground cinnamon

¼ tsp dried oregano

3 tbsp lemon hummus
 (see recipe on page 174)

2 tbsp pistachio pesto
 (see recipe on page 176)

½ handful fresh basil

I tsp toasted sesame seeds

Pepper

Heat 2 tablespoons of olive oil in a frying pan, add the bread and toast on both sides until golden brown. Finely dice the tomatoes and onion. First, sauté the onion in I tablespoon of oil for 5 minutes, then add the tomatoes. Add the balsamic vinegar glaze, salt, cinnamon and oregano. Lower the heat and leave everything to cook down.

In the meantime, spread hummus over the bread. Then top with the tomatoes and drizzle with pesto. Garnish with the fresh basil and sesame seeds, and season with freshly ground pepper.

WHEN YOUR BREAD GOES STALE
Has your bread gone stale again? No problem. Bruschetta is actually better when made with bread that isn't too fresh. And it doesn't matter whether you use white or brown bread. This combination is also heavenly on toast.

Couscous with sautéed vegetables

I love cooking for a living. Of course, there are also days when I just need to quickly satisfy my hunger. This couscous dish falls under the category of 'simple, but healthy and delicious'.

SERVES 2

100 g couscous

3 cloves garlic, chopped

1 onion, chopped

2 tbsp olive oil

½ leek

1 pepper

1 courgette

1 handful baby plum tomatoes

5 dried apricots

3 tbsp balsamic vinegar

1 tsp date syrup

1 tsp sambal oelek

1 tsp smoked paprika

¼ tsp ground caraway

¼ tsp ground coriander

Juice of 1 lemon

Salt and pepper

½ bunch parsley

Olive oil for drizzling

2 tbsp soya yoghurt, for
   serving

Cook the couscous in a saucepan of water according to the instructions on the packet. Heat the olive oil in a non-stick frying pan and sauté the garlic and onion well. Cut the vegetables into small pieces, add to the pan and sauté. Chop the apricots and add to the pan with the balsamic vinegar, date syrup, sambal oelek and all the spices. Then add the cooked couscous and season everything with lemon juice, salt and pepper.

Remove the pan from the heat, finely chop the parsley and gently stir into the couscous. Drizzle olive oil over the dish and serve lukewarm with a dollop of soya yoghurt.

Protein rissoles

MAKES 10–12

I courgette

I onion

½ bunch parsley

230 g cooked chickpeas

2 cloves garlic

I tsp paprika

½ tsp ground caraway

½ tsp ground coriander

I tsp salt

8 tbsp soya flour

2 tbsp olive oil

Olive oil, for cooking

For the dip

8 tbsp soya yoghurt

2 tbsp tahini

Juice of ½ lemon

¼ tsp garlic powder

½ tsp salt

Grate the courgette and set aside in a bowl. Chop the onion and parsley and combine with the chickpeas in a blender or food processor. Pulse in short bursts to form a slightly coarse and crumbly paste. Combine with the grated courgette in the bowl, then lightly stir in the remaining ingredients. Mix everything well, and use clean, cold hands to shape the mixture into rissoles. Fry these in a hot frying pan in olive oil on both sides for several minutes until golden brown.

For the dip, thoroughly mix all the ingredients. Serve the rissoles with a side salad and the dip.

Olive pesto focaccia panini

I was inspired to make this focaccia panini by a lovely experience we had in a small Italian village. It was lunchtime and we were hungry, so we went off to find panini. As there was nothing without meat on offer, the man behind the counter immediately went out of his way to prepare a delicious vegetable-filled panini. It tasted so good that it was given its place in this book. Sometimes the simplest combinations are the best.

SERVES 2

1 courgette

½ aubergine

2 tbsp olive oil

¼ tsp salt

2 tomatoes

2 focaccias (see basic recipe on page 37)

For the pesto

3 cloves garlic

1 small onion

6 tbsp olive oil

1 handful fresh basil

120 g pitted black olives

1 tbsp yeast flakes

Juice of ½ lemon

Salt and pepper

Thinly slice the courgette and aubergine along their length and fry the slices in the olive oil until golden brown. Season with salt.

For the pesto, chop the garlic and onion and sauté in a little oil. Use a stick blender to purée with the remaining oil, basil, olives and yeast flakes. Season with a little lemon juice, salt and pepper.

Slice the tomatoes. Cut the focaccias in half through the middle and spread the bottom half generously with pesto. Top with the tomato and lukewarm vegetable slices and cover with the top half. Cut the panini in half and serve immediately.

Green bean, onion and tempeh salad

Green beans are one of those foods that I like very much but would only rarely buy. Fortunately, Italy also changed me in this respect. I can never forget the delicious taste of green bean salad.

SERVES 2

300 g green beans

2 onions

2 tbsp olive oil

Salt and pepper

For the tempeh

125 g tempeh

2 tbsp soy sauce

1 tsp paprika

1 tsp garlic powder

1 tsp rice syrup

2 tsp olive oil

For the dressing

5 tbsp balsamic vinegar

2 tsp vegan mayonnaise

¼ tsp garlic powder

Juice of ½ lemon

3 tbsp olive oil

Top and tail the beans and simmer in a saucepan of boiling water for 15 minutes. Chop the onions and sauté in a frying pan with the oil.

In the meantime, cut the tempeh into small cubes. Make a marinade by mixing the remaining ingredients and coat the tempeh well.

When the beans are cooked, drain and set aside with the sautéed onions. In the same frying pan, fry the tempeh until crispy and golden brown, then combine in a bowl with the beans and onions.

Mix together the dressing ingredients. Add the dressing to the green bean salad and toss well. Season with salt and pepper and serve lukewarm.

OVEN RECIPES

Being on this trip has led me to devise more oven dishes that ever. The Omnia — my little oven I use on the hob — has been an absolute discovery. It might look like an oversized savarin cake tin, but it actually works quite like the oven you have at home. To enable you to cook all the dishes in this chapter both at home and on the road, two sets of instructions are provided for each recipe. They give the temperature and baking time for both a conventional oven and for an Omnia.

I especially recommend the potato, leek and fennel gratin, and the lentil moussaka.

Potato, leek and fennel gratin

There's nothing like a good gratin. We were particularly taken with the leek and fennel combination, even though Chris doesn't actually like fennel.

SERVES 2

5–6 floury potatoes

2 tbsp olive oil

1 leek

2 onions

1 fennel bulb

300 ml oat cream

1 ½ tbsp cashew butter

3 tbsp yeast flakes

¾ tsp garlic powder

½ tsp salt

1 handful freshly chopped parsley

Pepper

1 pinch freshly grated nutmeg

Without peeling, thinly slice the potatoes with a sharp knife. Brush an ovenproof dish (or Omnia pan) with the oil and arrange the potatoes inside. You can stack two to three layers of potatoes on top of each other. Then slice the leek and onions into fine rings and the fennel lengthways into thin strips. Spread the leek, onions and fennel over the potatoes.

In a bowl, whisk the oat cream with the cashew butter, yeast flakes, garlic powder and salt and pour the sauce evenly over the casserole. Bake in a convection oven at 200°C for about 40 minutes. If using an Omnia, this takes about the same amount of time on a high heat. Serve the gratin with the freshly chopped parsley, pepper and nutmeg.

A GOOD WAY TO REDUCE FOOD WASTE

A gratin is a wonderful way to use up vegetables that are past their prime. The combination of potatoes with carrots or courgettes is delicious. In this case, I grate the vegetables finely and cover the potato slices with them before cooking in the oven. This makes the vegetables nice and crispy.

Mediterranean Muffins

When it comes to snacks, I actually prefer them to be quite substantial. That's why I make sure to always keep a container with a hearty treat in our van fridge. I am particularly fond of these muffins, which are both fragrant and bursting with protein and vitamins.

MAKES 6

½ leek

½ pepper

1 courgette

6 baby plum tomatoes

3 cloves garlic, chopped

2 tbsp olive oil

1 tsp paprika

½ tsp salt

1 tsp Italian herbs

6 sun-dried tomatoes
   marinated in oil

8 pitted olives

Oil, for greasing

250 g silken tofu

50 g soya flour

½ tsp salt

½ tsp garlic powder

2 tbsp olive oil

10 g yeast flakes

Pepper

Slice the leek, pepper and courgette into thin strips and quarter the baby plum tomatoes. Sauté the vegetables in a frying pan with the oil and the chopped garlic. Add the herbs and spices. As soon as the vegetables turn golden brown, lower the heat. Cut the sun-dried tomatoes and olives into small pieces and stir into the vegetables. Remove the pan from the heat.

Blend the remaining ingredients together in a blender or food processor, or with a stick blender to a runny paste and stir into the vegetables (without blending). Divide the mixture into six (6.5 cm) greased muffin moulds. Bake the muffins in a convection oven at 180°C for about 25 minutes (if using an Omnia, bake on a medium heat for 30 minutes).

Leave the muffins to cool and develop their aroma overnight. They taste best cold the following day.

GIVE FREE REIN TO CREATIVITY
Don't hesitate to adapt this recipe to your own taste. Try making muffins with artichokes, sweetcorn, pine nuts and rocket, for instance, or just use whatever you find in the fridge. This is also an ideal way to use up overripe vegetables.

Lentil moussaka

During our time in Greece, we were always on the lookout for a vegan moussaka. Because we couldn't find what we were looking for, I devised my very own creation in my van kitchen. We used lentils instead of minced meat. The result is an aromatic and harmonious dish that is definitely one of my favourite recipes in this book.

SERVES 4

For the filling

2 large onions

2 tbsp olive oil

2 carrots

1 tbsp balsamic vinegar

1 tsp agave syrup

200 g whole brown lentils

350 ml water

350 ml tomato passata (sieved tomatoes)

1 tsp Italian herbs

1 tsp smoked paprika

1 tsp garlic powder

Salt and pepper

2 aubergines

5–6 tbsp olive oil

Oil, for greasing

For the sauce

350 ml soya cream

5 tsp yeast flakes

½ tsp garlic powder

2 dashes lemon juice

2 tsp plain flour

¾ tsp salt

Pepper

Chop the onions and sauté in a saucepan with the olive oil. Grate the carrots and add. Deglaze the pan with the balsamic vinegar, then add the agave syrup. Add the lentils and half of the water and cook until thickened. Then add the remaining water and passata. Season with the herbs and spices, lower the heat and simmer until the lentils are tender.

In the meantime, cut the aubergines along their length into 5-mm-thick slices and brush all over with olive oil. Fry in a non-stick frying pan until golden brown on both sides. Set aside.

For the sauce, combine the soya cream with the yeast flakes, garlic powder and lemon juice in a saucepan and bring to the boil. Sift the flour and sprinkle in. Stir well with a whisk to prevent lumps from forming. Allow the sauce to thicken and season with salt and pepper.

Grease an ovenproof dish or Omnia pan. Cover the bottom with a layer of aubergine slices, as if making lasagne, and cover with the lentils. Then make another aubergine layer and cover with the sauce. Repeat the process until the ingredients are used up. Save enough sauce to pour over the moussaka as a finishing touch.

Bake in a convection oven at 200°C for about 35 minutes. If using an Omnia, this takes the same amount of time on a medium heat. After baking, leave to stand for 10 minutes until the sauce firms up. Leave to cool and serve warm, not piping hot.

Gemista

Gemista is the name of a Greek dish made of stuffed tomatoes or peppers. They're typically filled with rice, but the vegetables are also filled with bulgur in some regions of Greece. Because we ate this dish whenever we would have a restaurant meal in Greece, I couldn't resist taking inspiration from it to make my very own version of Gemista.

SERVES 2

2 peppers

2 round courgettes

6 tbsp olive oil

1 onion, chopped

25 g pine nuts

1 cup cooked long grain rice

2 tsp tomato purée

1 tbsp balsamic vinegar

2 tomatoes

½ tsp salt

½ tsp smoked paprika

4 sprigs thyme

Pepper

1 handful freshly chopped parsley

Cut the tops off the peppers and courgettes and set aside. Remove the seeds from the peppers. Use a spoon to scoop out the courgette flesh and cut into small pieces. Heat some olive oil in a frying pan and sauté the onion. Add the pine nuts and courgette flesh and sauté. Add the rice, tomato purée and balsamic vinegar and simmer for a few minutes, stirring occasionally.

In the meantime, finely chop and strain the tomatoes. Add the tomatoes to the pan and cook down. Season with salt, paprika and fresh thyme leaves, followed by freshly ground pepper, then simmer for 10 more minutes.

Fill the peppers and courgettes with the rice mixture and replace their tops. Place the stuffed vegetables in an ovenproof dish and brush generously with olive oil. Bake in the oven at 180°C (upper and lower heat) for about 50 minutes. If using an Omnia, this takes about the same amount of time on a high heat. The vegetables are ready to come out as soon as the skin of the peppers blackens or blisters, which is when they develop a wonderful smoky aroma.

Serve sprinkled with the freshly chopped parsley. If you like, you can also drizzle over with a little freshly squeezed lemon juice and more olive oil.

FOR MORE VARIETY

The classic version of Gemista is stuffed tomatoes and courgettes, but you can also stuff aubergines. You rarely find round courgettes in supermarkets, but they are often available at local farmers' markets.

Butternut squash and sauerkraut lasagne with lemon-flavoured béchamel sauce

For me, the end of summer is always made less depressing by the prospect of winter squash season. I made this lasagne with the first butternut squash I could get my hands on, and it's been a favourite of mine ever since.

SERVES 3–4

For the lasagne

2 onions

2 cloves garlic

2 tbsp olive oil

1 butternut squash

100 g sunflower mince
   (or soya mince)

12 sage leaves, chopped

½ tsp dried oregano

½ tsp garlic powder

2 tsp date syrup (or other
   sweetener)

1 ½ tsp vegetable stock powder

150 ml water

300 g unpasteurised sauerkraut

1 handful rocket

250 ml oat cream

¾ tsp salt

Pepper

10–12 lasagne sheets

Olive oil, for greasing

For the béchamel sauce

50 g margarine

3 tsp light spelt flour

220 ml oat milk

6 tsp yeast flakes

Salt and pepper

Zest and juice of 1 lemon

Chop the onions and garlic and sauté in a frying pan with the olive oil. Dice the squash into bite-sized pieces and add. After sautéing for about 5 minutes, add the sunflower mince and season with sage, oregano, garlic powder and date syrup, stirring constantly. Dissolve the vegetable stock in the water and deglaze the pan. Add the sauerkraut and rocket and cook for 5 minutes, then add the oat cream. Lower the heat, season with salt and pepper and leave everything to cook down.

In the meantime, make the béchamel sauce. To do this, melt the margarine in a saucepan, add the flour and cook to a smooth paste, incorporating the oat milk. Sprinkle in the yeast flakes and season with salt and pepper. Finally, incorporate the lemon zest and lemon juice.

Grease an ovenproof dish with a little olive oil and line the bottom with lasagne sheets. Then make alternate layers of filling, sauce and lasagne sheets. Finish by covering with béchamel sauce. Bake the lasagne in the oven at 180°C (upper and lower heat) for about 30 minutes. If using an Omnia, this takes 10–15 minutes longer on a high heat.

FOR THAT SPECIAL TOUCH

If you like, sprinkle some seed blend over the sauce on top of the lasagne. The recipe is on page 34.

Stuffed Portobello mushrooms

Portobello mushrooms are nothing more than large white mushrooms. Okay, almost. The taste is definitely more aromatic, with more of an umami taste, which is why this mushroom is also often used as a meat substitute for burgers. In my recipe, these delicious mushrooms are stuffed and baked.

SERVES 2

5–6 Portobello mushrooms

3 tbsp olive oil

200 g tofu ricotta (see recipe on page 29)

Zest of 1 lemon

80 g green olives, finely chopped

¼ bunch parsley, freshly chopped

A few freshly chopped mint leaves

1 handful pine nuts

Pepper (optional)

Oil, for greasing

Carefully wipe the mushrooms clean and remove the stalks.

In a non-stick frying pan, fry the hollow mushroom caps in oil on both sides until lightly golden (about 8 minutes). In the meantime, prepare the filling. Mix the tofu ricotta with the lemon zest, olives and the chopped herbs in a bowl. Stuff the mushrooms with the tofu mixture, place on a lightly greased baking tray and bake in a convection oven at 200°C for 30 minutes. If using an Omnia, this takes about the same amount of time on a high heat.

Before serving, toast a few pine nuts in a frying pan, chop and sprinkle over the baked mushrooms. If you like a little more kick, you can also add some sambal oelek and season with freshly ground pepper.

IF IT'S NEVER SPICY ENOUGH

Sambal oelek can now be found in practically every supermarket. This thick chilli sauce was invented in Indonesia, where it is served with every dish. If you often like to eat spicy food, you can make this sauce yourself very easily. Simply boil chilli peppers and then purée them together with oil, salt and a little sugar.

Aubergine and tofu ricotta involtini

Involtini is the Italian word for a dish of small bundles wrapped around a filling. In Italy, however, involtini are typically made of meat. But this aubergine version is at least as delicious, especially when combined with home-made tofu ricotta.

SERVES 2

2 aubergines

5 tbsp olive oil

2 cloves garlic, chopped

1 red onion, finely chopped

400 ml tomato passata (sieved tomatoes)

5 tbsp balsamic vinegar

4 sprigs rosemary

150 g tofu ricotta (see recipe on page 29)

¼ tsp salt

Pepper

Oil, for greasing

Thinly slice the aubergines along their length with a sharp knife and brush all over with olive oil. In a frying pan, sauté all the aubergine strips on both sides in the olive oil for a few minutes until they can be easily shaped and rolled. Set aside. Sauté the garlic and onion in the same pan. After a few minutes, add the passata and balsamic vinegar. Then add the rosemary and leave everything to cook down on a low heat. In the meantime, spread each aubergine slice with tofu ricotta and roll up. Season the tomato sauce with salt and freshly ground pepper.

Pour the finished tomato sauce into a greased ovenproof dish or Omnia pan. Carefully arrange the involtini on the bed of sauce. Bake in a convection oven at 190°C for about 30 minutes. If using an Omnia, this takes about 35 minutes on a high heat.

WHEN TIME IS OF THE ESSENCE
If you don't have the time or inclination to make your own ricotta, you can simply use store-bought vegan cream cheese.

Double-sauced patatas bravas

People tend to associate patatas bravas with Spain. But it reminds me of a wonderful evening spent at Myrtos Beach on the Greek island of Kefalonia. There we enjoyed these delicious potatoes at sunset and with no other company but our own. Who knows? Perhaps this dish will also add a bit of the same holiday feeling to the cuisines of other places.

SERVES 2

5 medium potatoes
4 tbsp olive oil
I tsp salt
½ tsp dried rosemary
½ tsp garlic powder

For the smoked paprika sauce
I small red pepper
I tsp smoked paprika
Juice of ½ lemon
½ tsp garlic powder
I tsp pear concentrate
3 tsp tahini
2 tbsp vegan yoghurt
I tsp yeast flakes
Pepper

For the lemon and garlic sauce
2 tbsp hummus
4 tbsp vegan yoghurt
Zest of ½ lemon
30 ml plant-based milk
I clove garlic
I ½ tsp sambal oelek
  (or harissa)
Pepper

Extra
Freshly chopped parsley

Thoroughly wash and dice the unpeeled potatoes and mix in a bowl with the olive oil, salt, rosemary and garlic. Roast in a preheated convection oven at 220°C for about 30 minutes until golden brown. If using an Omnia, this takes the same amount of time on a high heat. Turn the potato pieces over from time to time so that they become crispy on all sides.

In the meantime, make the two sauces. Blend all the ingredients in a blender or food processor, or with a stick blender until smooth. Once the patatas bravas are cooked through and golden brown, transfer to a serving dish. Spread the two sauces over the top with a spoon.

The dish tastes great with freshly chopped parsley. We like to use any leftover sauce the next day as a dip for bread, or as a pasta sauce.

REDUCE FOOD WASTE
If you have any cooked potatoes leftover from the previous day, you can also cut them into cubes and fry them in a pan until crispy, instead of using the oven. This is a practical and time-saving option that reduces food waste.

Oven-baked ratatouille with béchamel sauce

This stewed vegetable dish is to die for. Originally meaning 'stirred food', ratatouille got its name because the stew was often cooked for hours. In fact, it's one of those dishes that gets even better with every reheating. Except that we've never managed to have any leftovers to reheat.

SERVES 2

For the ratatouille

1 large courgette

1 aubergine

3 tomatoes

2 red onions

400 g tin chopped tomatoes

½ tsp dried oregano

¾ tsp garlic powder

½ tsp salt

Pepper

Oil, for greasing

10–15 basil leaves, for garnishing

For the béchamel sauce

50 g margarine

3 tsp plain flour

220 ml oat milk

6 tsp yeast flakes

Salt and pepper

Cut the courgettes, aubergine and fresh tomatoes into slices of uniform thickness (about 5 mm).

Arrange the slices alternately in a well-greased ovenproof dish (or Omnia pan), filling the entire dish. Cut the onions into eighths and insert them into gaps between the vegetables. Mix the chopped tomatoes with the oregano and garlic powder and season with salt and pepper. Pour over the vegetables and spread evenly.

For the béchamel sauce, melt the margarine in a saucepan, add the flour and cook to a smooth paste, incorporating the oat milk. Add the yeast flakes and season with salt and pepper. Then pour the sauce over the ratatouille and bake in the oven at 180°C (upper and lower heat) for about 30 minutes. If using an Omnia, this takes 40 minutes on a high heat.

Serve the baked ratatouille hot, garnished with the fresh basil.

FOR EVEN MORE AROMA
The flavour of the stew can be even more intense if seasoned with fresh thyme or rosemary sprigs before baking, or if you cook the tomato sauce from scratch.

AFTER HOURS

These recipes are for anyone who likes to take a little extra time to cook something delicious after a day's work or at weekends. Don't worry, though; you won't need to spend hours in the kitchen to make any of these dishes. But sometimes good things take time. The creamy mushroom soup, in particular, will only develop its great aroma when allowed to simmer for a little longer. And the flavour of winter squash is richer when cooked very well. Hopefully, this chapter will appeal to anyone who likes to try out new combinations and let off a little steam in the kitchen.

Creamy mushroom and oat soup

This soup is a dish to warm the soul. It's also a balanced meal that contains vitamins from the different vegetables, proteins from the beans and long-chain carbohydrates from the wholegrain oats. The mushrooms also add an earthy umami taste to the dish.

SERVES 2

1 onion

3 cloves garlic

2 tbsp olive oil

15 g dried porcini mushrooms

10 sun-dried tomatoes

120 g fresh shiitake mushrooms

1 carrot

¼ head broccoli

5 sprigs fresh thyme

½ tsp dried oregano

1 ½ tsp vegetable stock powder

350 ml water

100 g oat groats

200 ml soya cream

150 g cooked haricot beans

1 ½ tbsp yeast flakes

Bread

1 handful freshly chopped basil

Pepper

Chop the onion and garlic and sauté in a saucepan with the oil. Soak the porcini mushrooms in lukewarm water to rehydrate. Slice the sun-dried tomatoes and the shiitake mushrooms into strips. Halve the carrot lengthways and then slice. Cut the broccoli into bite-sized pieces. Add all the vegetables and mushrooms to the pan and sauté. Stir in the thyme and oregano.

Dissolve the vegetable stock in the water and deglaze the pan. Add the oat groats and lower the heat, then cover the pan and leave everything to cook down. After about 15 minutes, add the soya cream, beans and yeast flakes. Bring everything to the boil again for 5 minutes, then serve garnished with freshly chopped basil, seasoned with freshly ground pepper and with a slice of bread.

Pasta with miso, aubergine and pesto

This pasta recipe came about as we were setting off on our trip to Greece. It wasn't actually intended to be included in the cookbook, but as is so often the case, improvised dishes are often the best. Because Chris was so enthusiastic about the dish, even though he isn't normally a big fan of aubergines, it has now found a well-deserved place in *Vegan Camper Van Cooking*.

SERVES 2

1 red onion

2 cloves garlic

2 tbsp olive oil

2 medium aubergines

1 courgette

1½ tsp miso paste

¾ tsp smoked paprika

2 tsp sugar (or other sweetener)

3 tbsp balsamic vinegar

1 tbsp pesto

½ tsp salt

Water, as needed

250 g pasta of your choice

Juice of ½ lemon

1 handful walnut kernels

5–6 lovage leaves

Pepper

Chop the onion and garlic and sauté in a frying pan with the olive oil until golden brown.

Halve the aubergines and courgettes and cut lengthways into 5-mm-thick slices. Add both to the pan and sauté. After 7–10 minutes, add the miso paste, paprika and sugar and cook until the sugar is lightly caramelised. Deglaze the pan with the balsamic vinegar and lower the heat. Stir in the pesto and season everything with salt. Continue to simmer the vegetables, stirring occasionally. Depending on the pan you use, add a little water to stop the vegetables from drying out.

In the meantime, cook the pasta according to the instructions on the packet. When the pasta is ready, drizzle the lemon juice over the vegetables. Divide the pasta into two plates and top with the vegetables. Chop the walnuts, slice the lovage into strips and sprinkle both over the pasta. Season with freshly ground pepper and serve hot.

IF YOU'RE FEELING MORE AMBITIOUS
If you have more time, enjoy this pasta with home-made tofu ricotta (page 29). Its creaminess really enhances the dish, and the high protein content of the tofu improves its nutritional values. Combining carbohydrates with proteins in one meal has been shown to keep you fuller for longer.

Pot barley with squash and chestnuts

This dish showcases all the beauty of autumn in one pan. Pot barley is also given the attention it deserves. It doesn't always have to be rice, pasta or quinoa.

SERVES 2

¾ cup pot barley

Water

200 g tofu

1 tsp miso paste

10 tsp soy sauce

1 onion

1 tbsp olive oil

1 small red kuri squash

100 g cooked chestnuts

¾ tsp garlic powder

¼ tsp cumin seeds

1 tsp smoked paprika

2 tsp hot mustard

200 ml soya cream

150 ml water

Juice of ½ lemon

1 handful raisins

Salt and pepper

Freshly chopped parsley, for garnishing

Cook the pot barley in three times its volume of water according to the instructions on the packet.

Cut the tofu into cubes and marinate in a mixture of the miso paste with the soy sauce. Chop the onion and sauté in a frying pan with the oil for a few minutes. Peel, de-seed and cut the squash into bite-sized pieces. Add to the pan and sauté. Add the tofu and sauté everything until golden brown. Then add the chestnuts, spices and mustard. Finally, add the soya cream and water and leave everything to cook down on a low heat. Once the squash is tender, add the lemon juice and raisins. Season with pepper and salt.

Put the cooked pot barley on plates and spread the contents of the pan over the top. Garnish with freshly chopped parsley and serve.

DRAWING EVEN MORE ATTENTION TO HERITAGE GRAINS
Cooked buckwheat, oat groats and green spelt also make excellent accompaniments for the squash and chestnuts.

Protein burritos

These burritos are perfect for a quick lunch or dinner. The great thing about them is that the recipe can be adapted to suit the time you have and your inclination to cook.

SERVES 2 (MAKES 4 BURRITOS)

For the filling

2 cloves garlic

1 red onion

1 tbsp olive oil

1 red pepper

50 g sunflower mince (or soya mince)

1 ½ tsp smoked paprika

Chilli powder

½ tsp dried herbs (oregano, basil, thyme)

¾ tsp salt

2 tomatoes

1 ½ tsp balsamic glaze

150 g sweetcorn

150 g cooked kidney beans (or black beans)

1 tsp pear concentrate (or other sweetener)

Extras

5 tbsp lemon hummus (see recipe on page 174)

Fresh mint and parsley

4 large tortilla wraps

2 handfuls cooked rice from the previous day

Chop the garlic and onion and sauté in a frying pan with the olive oil. De-seed and slice the pepper into thin strips and add to the pan. Add the sunflower mince and season well with paprika, chilli powder, dried herbs and salt. Sauté for 5 more minutes, stirring constantly, then chop the tomatoes into chunks and add. Next, add the balsamic glaze, sweetcorn and beans and sauté together. Finally, add the pear concentrate and leave to simmer for about 10 minutes.

In the meantime, make the hummus as described on page 174. Chop some fresh mint and parsley. Now fill the tortillas: first spread the rice in a line over the middle of the tortilla wraps, then top with the filling. Follow this with the hummus and freshly chopped herbs. Carefully roll up the burrito tightly and cut in half. Garnish with the remaining fresh herbs and serve lukewarm.

FOR ADDED PROTEIN

If you have more time and crave even more protein, you can also easily make tortilla wraps yourself. You only need two ingredients: red lentils and water. Cook the lentils until soft, then blend with the water to make a batter. Fry the tortillas in a pan with oil, just like making pancakes.

Baked sweet potato with lentil dhal

Dhal (also spelt as dal and daal) is a traditional Indian dish that is served with almost every main meal in India. We haven't got that far in the van yet, but Asian cuisines inspire me like no other, even on the road. I find this spicy dhal tastes particularly good with sweet potatoes.

SERVES 2

2 large sweet potatoes

2 tbsp olive oil

2 onions

3 cloves garlic

1 ½–2-cm length fresh ginger

1 tsp turmeric powder

½ tsp ground coriander

1 tsp cumin seeds

200 g red lentils

450 ml vegetable stock

200 ml oat cream

2 tomatoes, chopped

50 g raisins

3 tbsp tomato purée

2 tsp sugar

3 tbsp lemon juice

2 tbsp tofu ricotta (see recipe on page 29) (optional)

Thoroughly wash and dry the sweet potatoes. Prick several times with a fork and then bake in a convection oven at 190°C for about 50 minutes, until fully cooked. If using an Omnia, this takes about the same amount of time on a high heat. Use a fork to check whether the sweet potatoes are cooked through.

In the meantime, make the dhal. Heat the olive oil in a saucepan. Finely chop the onions and garlic cloves and sauté in the pan. Also finely chop the ginger and add. Then fry all the spices so that they can release all their aromas. Rinse the lentils in cold water and then add them to the pan. Pour in the vegetable stock and bring to the boil. Stir well, cover and simmer for 10 minutes. Once the lentils have absorbed most of the liquid, add the oat cream, chopped tomatoes, raisins and tomato purée. Season with the sugar and lemon juice. The dhal tastes best when it is left to simmer for 20–30 more minutes. Only then do all the spice flavours really develop.

The dhal is served inside a sweet potato. To do this, carefully make a cut lengthways down the centre and fill with dhal. Top with tofu ricotta if you like. Fresh coriander and/or a little vegan yoghurt also go well with this dish.

FOR EVEN MORE GOOD PROTEINS

The classic dhal is made with lentils. But the dish is just as delicious when made using other pulses, such as beans or chickpeas. This not only adds variety to your diet, but also ensures that all the essential amino acids can be covered together in a single vegan meal.

Cauliflower and potato soup

On our trip to Italy, we unexpectedly ended up in the beautiful region of Abruzzo. However, evenings can also get really cold there in early October, so a piping hot soup was very welcome. What makes this recipe special is that all the ingredients are roasted in the oven beforehand. This dish will keep you warm all through the winter.

SERVES 2

1 cauliflower
2 potatoes
1 small onion
2 cloves garlic
2 tbsp olive oil
½ tsp salt
400 ml vegetable stock
80 ml soya cream
1 tbsp yeast flakes
1 pinch ground caraway
2 pinches freshly grated nutmeg
Salt and pepper

For the toppings
1 handful cauliflower florets (see method)
1 tsp olive oil
⅓ tsp turmeric powder
¼ tsp salt
1 handful cashew nuts
½ pomegranate
Fresh mint

Divide the cauliflower into florets and set aside a handful for the topping. Peel and cut the potatoes into bite-sized pieces. Quarter the onion and garlic. Put everything together on a baking tray and mix with the oil and salt. Roast in a convection oven at 200°C for about 25 minutes, until the vegetables are cooked through. If using an Omnia, this takes a few minutes longer on a high heat.

In a frying pan, sauté the cauliflower florets, previously set aside, in the oil, season and add the cashews. Turn off the heat as soon as the nuts are golden brown. Scoop out the pomegranate seeds and chop some fresh mint.

Use a blender or food processor, or stick blender to blend the roasted vegetables with the vegetable stock and soya cream to make the soup. Add more stock if the soup becomes too thick. Transfer to a large saucepan and season with yeast flakes, caraway seeds, nutmeg, salt and pepper. Bring everything to the boil again, stirring constantly, so that the soup can be served hot.

Garnish the soup with the different topping ingredients and serve immediately.

Penne with balsamic vinegar

Many people are probably only familiar with balsamic vinegar in salads, which is a pity, really. Especially for pasta dishes, this sweet and sour vinegar is an absolute eye-opener.

SERVES 2

250 g penne

1 onion

1 tbsp olive oil

6 chestnut mushrooms

1 raw beetroot

100 ml balsamic vinegar

3 tsp pear concentrate

1 tsp vegetable stock powder

6 sprigs thyme

2 pinches salt

Pepper

½ tsp smoked paprika

100 g cashew cheese

Spring onions, finely chopped

Cook the penne according to the instructions on the packet, then pour off the water and leave to drain. Chop the onion and sauté in a frying pan with the olive oil. In the meantime, clean and slice the mushrooms and add to the sautéed onion. Dice the beetroot. Remove the mushrooms from the pan and set aside. Add the balsamic vinegar and pear concentrate to the pan and bring to the boil. Lower the heat and add the beetroot. Season with the vegetable stock powder. Pluck the thyme and add. Simmer for 10 more minutes, until the sauce caramelises. Season with salt and freshly ground pepper.

Add the mushrooms and the pasta to the sauce in the pan, season with paprika powder and mix everything well. Cut the cashew cheese into bite-sized pieces and add to the pan. Serve the dish with some finely chopped spring onions.

WHAT MAKES A GOOD BALSAMIC VINEGAR

Balsamic vinegar is a vinegar that originated in the region around the Italian city of Modena. A good balsamic vinegar tastes more sweetish than sour, with an intense and aromatic flavour. When choosing balsamic vinegar, it's best not to pick the cheapest variety; instead, you should pay attention to the acidity. Ideally, this should be 6–6.5 per cent.

Lukewarm summer rolls

Summer rolls are one of my favourite starters, but not just in summer. Because of this, not all the ingredients that are wrapped in the rice paper are raw, which is often the case in the original Vietnamese recipe. Tofu, aubergine and mushrooms can go into the pan first. The rolls are then served lukewarm.

SERVES 2

200 g tofu

3 tbsp sesame oil

5 tbsp soy sauce

15 shiitake mushrooms

1 aubergine

2 carrots

1 cucumber

1 handful fresh mint

1 handful fresh coriander

12–14 rice paper wrappers

For the dipping sauce

3 tbsp vegan mayonnaise

1 tbsp soy sauce

1-cm length fresh ginger, grated

Juice of ½ lime

1 tsp rice syrup

½ tsp garlic powder

Dash water

Drain the tofu, wrap in a clean cloth and squeeze. Cut the block into thin strips about 5 mm thick and marinate in a mixture of the sesame oil and soy sauce. Sauté in a frying pan until golden brown on all sides.

In the meantime, cut the shiitake mushrooms and the aubergine into thin strips. Remove the tofu from the pan and set aside. Sauté the mushrooms and aubergine in the same pan. Cut the carrots and cucumber into even thinner batons and set aside. Chop the fresh herbs.

Assemble all the prepared filling ingredients next to each other on a chopping board. Dip one rice paper wrapper at a time in a bowl of lukewarm water. Place tofu, raw vegetables, aubergine, mushrooms and fresh herbs on a wrapper. Lift the bottom edge of the wrapper over the filling and fold the right and left sides inwards. Then roll up from the bottom to the top, ensuring the filling is completely enclosed. Repeat the process until all the ingredients have been used up. Finally, cut the rolls in half through the middle.

For the dipping sauce, mix all the ingredients together in a small mixing bowl and drizzle a little over the rolls. Put the remainder into a bowl to accompany the summer rolls. Serve the rolls lukewarm.

MORE DIPPING SAUCE IDEAS
Summer rolls are typically accompanied by soy sauce or a peanut dipping sauce. You can find a recipe for a peanut and ginger sauce on page 176.

Noodle and tofu boats

This recipe is inspired by a classic Thai dish, pad Thai. I like to serve this rice noodle dish in large lettuce leaves. This way, you can either eat the filling using cutlery or roll up the leaf and eat it with your hands.

SERVES 2

200 g rice noodles

2 tbsp sesame oil

4–6 lettuce leaves

150 g tofu

¼ tsp salt

I pepper

2 carrots

I tbsp peanut butter

5 tbsp soy sauce

5 tbsp water

I-cm length fresh ginger

I clove garlic

2 tsp sweetener of choice

Juice of I lemon

¼ tsp chilli powder

I handful chopped peanuts

I handful freshly chopped coriander

Cook the rice noodles according to the instructions on the packet, then toss in a little oil and set aside.

Wash and dry the lettuce leaves well.

Cut the tofu into cubes and sauté in a pan with the remaining oil and a little salt until crispy on all sides. Cut the pepper and carrots into fine strips, add to the pan and sauté for 5 more minutes.

Use a blender or food processor, or stick blender to blend the peanut butter, soy sauce, water, ginger, garlic, sweetener, lemon juice and chilli powder into a sauce. Add the rice noodles to the pan with the tofu and vegetables. Pour the sauce over and mix everything well.

Serve the noodles lukewarm on the lettuce leaves garnished with chopped peanuts and coriander.

Spaghetti with creamy chanterelle sauce

You won't believe the mushrooms we found in Sweden! When my brother came with his tent to pay us a visit, we would go looking for fresh mushrooms to pick every day. For us, this was an absolute highlight of our time there, and it also brought back fond childhood memories. We quite often used to walk through the woods with our dad in late summer. And in the evening we would always have pasta with a creamy mushroom sauce.

SERVES 2

350 g chanterelle mushrooms

3 tbsp olive oil

2 shallots

80 g smoked tofu

½ tsp salt

Pepper

3 tbsp white wine

200 ml oat cream

I tsp plain flour

250 g spaghetti

½ bunch chives

Clean the chanterelles (wash and dry if necessary) and cut in half. Heat the oil in a frying pan and sauté the mushrooms.

Finely chop the shallots, cut the tofu into very small cubes and sauté with the mushrooms. Season with salt and a little pepper. Deglaze the pan with the white wine, add the cream and leave to cook down. Mix the flour with a little water until smooth, to prevent lumps forming in the sauce, and pour the mixture into the pan. The sauce will thicken when it comes to the boil.

In the meantime, cook the spaghetti according to instructions on the packet, then pour off the water and leave to drain. Then add the spaghetti to the mushrooms and lower the heat. Finely chop the chives and season the sauce again. Serve the spaghetti with plenty of sauce and garnish with freshly chopped chives.

CLEAN CHANTERELLES PROPERLY
Mushrooms quickly become waterlogged when washed and lose their flavour, which is why it's better to clean the chanterelles by hand. A kitchen brush is the best utensil to use for this purpose. In an emergency, however, a soft toothbrush will also work.

Gnocchi with roasted pepper sauce

Peppers are a vegetable that I don't like at all when raw, but roasted peppers blow my mind. This is exactly why this sauce was such a discovery for me.

SERVES 2

For the gnocchi
Basic recipe on page 148
For the sauce
2 red peppers
1 tbsp olive oil
2 cloves garlic
¾ tsp smoked paprika
200 ml oat cream (or other vegan cream)
Juice of ½ lemon
½ tsp salt
Pepper

For the nut blend
150 g hazelnuts (or almonds)
5 tbsp yeast flakes
1 tsp garlic powder
½ tsp sweet paprika
2 tbsp olive oil
Salt and pepper

For the nut blend, grind the nuts in a blender or food processor, then mix with the remaining ingredients in a bowl. Stir well and store in the fridge. The mixture will keep for a fortnight.

For the sauce, quarter the peppers, remove the seeds and brush with the olive oil. Peel the garlic cloves and roast them whole together with the peppers in a convection oven at 200°C for about 30 minutes (or until the skin of the peppers blisters or blackens). Then combine the peppers and garlic cloves with the rest of the ingredients in the blender and blend to a creamy sauce (you can also use a stick blender for this). If using an Omnia, this takes about 35 minutes on a high heat.

Make the gnocchi as described in the recipe on page 148. Mix the gnocchi with the sauce, sprinkle with the nut blend and serve hot.

MAKE A VEGAN GRATED CHEESE ALTERNATIVE FROM SEEDS
Nut blend is not the only thing that goes well with this dish. Also be sure to try my seed blend (recipe on page 34).

Melon and courgette piadina

A piadina is the ideal lunch to have on the go. On our trip through Italy, street vendors were selling piadina, flatbread sandwiches, everywhere we went. The vegan version, unfortunately, often came with an avocado filling. Yet Italy, in particular, is a country with so many regional ingredients that are much more exciting. And that's how my melon and courgette piadina came about.

MAKES 4

For the flatbreads
300 g light spelt flour
150 ml warm water
30 ml olive oil
I level tsp salt
Oil, for cooking
Pepper

For the filling
2 courgettes
½ honeydew melon
2 tbsp olive oil
Salt and pepper
300 g tofu ricotta
  (see recipe on page 29)
Freshly chopped parsley

To make the flatbreads, mix all the ingredients in a bowl and knead for 5 minutes to form a dough. Cover the dough with a cloth and leave to rise for 20 minutes.

In the meantime, thinly slice the unpeeled courgettes along their length. Halve the melon, remove the seeds and also cut into slices. In a frying pan with the olive oil, sear the melon and courgette slices on both sides and season with salt and pepper.

Divide the dough into four equal-sized balls and flatten each portion into an oval about 3 mm thick. Cook each flatbread in a non-stick pan with a little oil for 2 minutes on both sides.

Spread the tofu ricotta over the flatbreads, then arrange the pan-seared courgette and melon slices on top and sprinkle freshly chopped parsley. Season the piadina with freshly ground pepper and serve lukewarm.

MORE IDEAS FOR PIADINA WITH A TWIST
Other delicious combinations include hummus with grilled vegetables, olives and rocket, and ricotta with caramelised walnuts and baked pear. There are really no limits to your imagination.

Pesto rosso risotto

During our trip through Italy, we only managed to spend a little time in the north of the country, and we completely missed out on the risotto region. To compensate, we often had risotto made in the van kitchen while we were on the road, which was a change from pizza and pasta.

SERVES 2

1 onion

Olive oil

1 cup risotto rice

1 dash white wine

2 cups water

1 ½ tsp salt

1 handful baby plum tomatoes

3 tsp organic pesto rosso

½ tsp garlic powder

½ tsp smoked paprika

Pepper

2 tsp yeast flakes

Juice of ½ lemon

1 handful chopped pistachio nuts

1 sprig basil, freshly chopped

Chop the onion and sauté in a saucepan with the olive oil. Add the rice and deglaze the pan with the white wine. Add the water and season with salt. Cover, lower the heat and stir from time to time. In the meantime, sauté the tomatoes in a frying pan with a little olive oil. When the risotto has absorbed two thirds of the liquid, add the pesto, spices, yeast flakes and lemon juice to the rice. Leave briefly for the flavours to infuse.

Once the risotto is cooked, arrange on plates with the sautéed tomatoes and serve garnished with chopped pistachios and basil.

MAKE YOUR OWN PESTO ROSSO
Pesto rosso is very easy to make yourself. Blend pine nuts and sun-dried tomatoes marinated in oil with garlic, yeast flakes, a little chilli, salt and pepper to a paste.

Gnocchi with tomato and saffron

Did you know that saffron is grown in many regions in Italy? Naturally, I couldn't help but buy a tin of those golden threads too. The result is a very simple dish that showcases two of the stars of Italian cuisine.

SERVES 2

500 g waxy potatoes

Salt

About 175 g light spelt flour or alternatively gluten-free flour

3 cloves garlic

1 tbsp olive oil

½ jar marinated tomatoes, halved

0.5 g saffron threads

Pepper

2 sprigs parsley, freshly chopped

To make the gnocchi, boil the unpeeled potatoes in salted water until tender. Peel, leave to cool and then mash the potatoes. Add the flour and three-quarters of a teaspoon of salt and knead into the mashed potatoes. Add more flour if the dough is too sticky. Roll the dough into 1½-cm thick cylinders and cut off 2-cm lengths with a knife. Give the gnocchi their typical shape and pattern by pressing them lightly on a fork.

Cook the gnocchi in a saucepan of hot salted water for a few minutes, until they float to the top, then scoop them out and leave to drain.

Chop the garlic and sauté in a frying pan with the oil. Add the gnocchi and the tomatoes. Sauté everything for several minutes, until golden brown. After a few minutes, add the saffron threads and season with salt and pepper.

This gnocchi dish tastes especially good with home-made vegan feta cheese (see page 30) and some fresh parsley.

DESSERTS

Unlike many of the other dishes in this book, the recipes in this section have not only been tested by Chris and myself. Quite often, after baking, we would meet new people with whom we could share these treats. The smell of freshly baked cakes would typically waft as far as the camper van beside us, and so these sweet treats were often the starting point for really interesting encounters. However, the tiramisu — my absolute favourite recipe from this section — doesn't even need baking. And the chokladbollar, Swedish chocolate and oat balls, are also quick and easy to make.

Plum cheesecake with streusel

There's simply nothing like crumbly streusel cakes. I don't remember how many times I baked this during the plum season. Even in my little van kitchen, this cake is super easy to prepare.

FOR AN OVENPROOF DISH OF ABOUT 25 × 25 CM

For the streusel
85 g chestnut flour
80 g light spelt flour or alternatively oat flour
70 g ground almonds
1 tsp linseed, coarsely ground
35 g sugar
2 tsp ground cinnamon
1 pinch salt
2 pinches ground cardamom
1 pinch ground cloves
35 ml rapeseed oil
60 ml water
20 ml oat milk
30 ml agave syrup
Oil, for greasing

For the filling
250 g soya yoghurt
Zest of ½ lemon
20 g sugar
350 g plums

To make the streusel, mix all the dry ingredients together in a bowl. Then add the wet ingredients, including the agave syrup, to the bowl and work everything into a crumbly dough. For best results, use cold hands.

For the filling, mix the soya yoghurt with the lemon zest and sugar in a separate bowl and set aside.

To make the base, spread two-thirds of the streusel over the bottom of a greased ovenproof dish and press down well with a silicone scraper or spatula. Cover with the filling. De-stone and quarter the plums and arrange them over the filling. Spread the last third of the streusel over the plums.

Bake the cake in a convection oven at 180°C for about 25 minutes. If using an Omnia, this takes about 30 minutes on a medium heat. This cake tastes best if left in the fridge overnight.

USE SEASONAL FRUITS

Instead of plums, you can make this cake with any fruits that are in season. It tastes absolutely delicious with tart apples in winter, fresh rhubarb in spring and raspberries in summer, to name a few.

Brownie muffins

These muffins live up to their name. While light and fluffy like muffins, they're also lovely and moist like brownies. Why should you have to choose when you can have both?

MAKES 6

120 g oat flour

100 g ground almonds

60 g sugar

30 g unsweetened cocoa powder

1 tsp linseed, coarsely ground

2 pinches ground cinnamon

1 pinch salt

1 tsp baking powder

60 g dark chocolate, chopped

250 g courgette, grated

30 ml rice syrup

20 ml rapeseed oil

110 ml soya cream

Oil, for greasing

Combine all the dry ingredients in a bowl, then add the wet ingredients and mix. Don't work the dough too much so that it retains air. Divide the dough between six (6.5 cm) greased ramekins and bake in a convection oven at 180°C for about 22 minutes. If using an Omnia, this takes about 10 minutes longer on a medium heat. The muffins won't be very firm straight after baking, but they have the perfect consistency after cooling down. They taste best if left in the fridge overnight.

TWO ARE BETTER THAN ONE
If you prefer, you can also make double the amount of the mixture and use it to bake brownies instead of muffins.

Cookie dough balls

Chris and I lead very active lives. Before doing sport, we like to build up our energy reserves with a small snack. These cookie dough balls — which really do taste like the real thing — are great for this.

MAKES 10–12

180 g cooked haricot beans

35 g almond butter
  (or peanut butter)

¼ tsp Bourbon vanilla powder

20 g coconut flour
  (or oat flour)

25 g date sugar

10 g sugar

1 pinch ground cinnamon

1 pinch salt

15 g cocoa nibs

70 g vegan dark chocolate

Rinse the cooked beans and leave to drain. Blend them together with the almond butter and vanilla powder in a blender or food processor, or with a stick blender until creamy. Then mix in a bowl with the coconut flour, date sugar, sugar, cinnamon and salt. Incorporate the cocoa nibs into the dough. Refrigerate for 30 minutes.

In the meantime, melt the chocolate over a bain-marie. Use a teaspoon to scoop out portions of dough and shape them into round balls with cold, dry hands. Coat the balls with melted chocolate and refrigerate until firm. Stored in an airtight container in the fridge, the cookie dough balls will keep for five days.

COOKIE DOUGH CAN ALSO BE EATEN WITH A SPOON
You don't really have to shape the cookie dough into balls; you can simply enjoy it as is with a spoon. You can also use cooked chickpeas instead of beans. However, they need to be rinsed thoroughly or the dough will taste strongly of chickpeas.

Chokladbollar

Chokladbollar are oat and chocolate balls that can be found in every bakery in Sweden. They are often totally vegan and are made with margarine instead of butter. I use nut butter as the source of fat for my own version, which I think tastes even better.

MAKES ABOUT 10

200 g Mazafati or other soft dates

120 g rolled oats

4 tbsp cocoa powder

50 g sugar

2 tbsp cashew butter

5 tbsp freshly brewed coffee

1 pinch salt

120 g dessicated coconut

Pit the dates and chop them finely. Grind the oats to a powder in a blender or food processor. Mix the dates with the oat flour in a bowl and knead with the remaining ingredients, except the dessicated coconut, with clean, cold hands to make a sticky dough. If you use other kinds of dates, make the dough in a food processor or soak them in hot water before use. If the dough is too dry, moisten it with a little more coffee or water.

Wash your hands before rolling the dough into about ten uniform balls. Roll the finished balls in dessicated coconut and store in the fridge. They taste best if left in the fridge for at least one night.

REPLACE THE COFFEE
If you don't like coffee, you can simply replace it with orange juice for a flavour that's equally good. The combination of 1 tablespoon of Cointreau with 4 tablespoons of orange juice is exquisite.

Tiramisu

If I had to choose a favourite dessert, it would most likely be tiramisu, which is why it's one of the first dishes I decided to veganise straight after I changed my diet over six years ago. I guess it's high time I shared this recipe with everyone.

SERVES 6–8

400 g silken tofu

I tsp psyllium husk powder (or a little whipped cream stabiliser)

5 tbsp sugar

250 ml soya-based whipping cream

Zest of ½ lemon

I pinch Bourbon vanilla powder

I pinch salt

350 g vegan biscuits

300 ml cold espresso coffee

3 tbsp amaretto

Cocoa powder, for dusting

Mix the tofu, psyllium husks and sugar in a stand mixer or with a hand mixer until fluffy. Whip the cream to stiff peaks and carefully fold into the tofu mixture together with the lemon zest, vanilla and salt. Set aside in the fridge.

Wrap the biscuits in a clean cloth and coarsely crush with a rolling pin. Spread the crumbs in a square baking tin and pour the coffee and amaretto over them. Press lightly to compact. Now spread the cream over the biscuit base and chill the tiramisu in the fridge for a few hours. Dust with cocoa powder before serving.

REPLACE THE COFFEE WITH RASPBERRIES
If you don't like coffee or would like to try a fruity version of tiramisu, you can cook down frozen raspberries in a saucepan and pour them over the biscuit base instead of the espresso and amaretto.

Stuffed dates

The fridge in our little van kitchen has a freezer compartment. It isn't very big, but there's always room inside for these snacks. I like to snack on stuffed dates in the evening while I listen to podcasts, or during the day whenever I feel peckish.

MAKES 10

10 pitted Medjool dates

10 tsp almond butter

1 pinch salt

¼ tsp ground cinnamon

60 g vegan dark chocolate

35 g chopped almonds

Cut the dates open along their length, fill them with almond butter and sprinkle them with salt and cinnamon. Melt the chocolate over a bain-marie and coat the dates with it. Sprinkle with chopped almonds. Put the dates in the fridge until the chocolate hardens.

Stored in an airtight container, these stuffed dates will easily keep for two weeks in the fridge and longer in the freezer. Leave them to thaw out briefly before eating.

FOR ALL PEANUT LOVERS
The dates are also delicious with a peanut butter filling and chopped peanuts. Then they even remind me a little of a Snickers bar.

Chocolate mousse

The chocolate mousse recipe featured in my first cookbook *Eat Your Greens!* was modestly named 'world's best chocolate mousse'. I think that this new version also lives up to the name, particularly because its main ingredient is sweet potatoes, which you wouldn't expect to find in a mousse.

SERVES 3–4

380 g sweet potatoes

130 g silken tofu

35 g vegan chocolate spread

30 g sugar

25 g cocoa powder

55 ml soya cream

1 pinch salt

1 pinch vanilla powder

Thoroughly wash and dry the unpeeled sweet potatoes. Prick several times with a fork and then bake in a convection oven at 200°C for about 50 minutes, until fully cooked. If using an Omnia, this takes a little longer. Then peel the sweet potatoes and blend the flesh with the remaining ingredients in a blender or food processor, or with a stick blender until creamy.

Divide the mousse between three or four glasses and refrigerate for at least 3 hours. Serve with vegan whipped cream or fresh fruit.

Cinnamon and cardamom buns

There's nothing quite like the smell of freshly baked yeast-leavened pastries! On our trip through Sweden, we treated ourselves to kannelbullar, cinnamon buns, at every opportunity. But even more than the classic cinnamon buns, I liked the cinnamon and cardamom buns even more.

MAKES 6–8

For the dough
550 g light spelt flour
1 ½ tsp salt
21 g fresh yeast
5 tsp sugar
70 g vegan butter
300 ml oat milk
Flour, for dusting
Oil, for greasing

For the filling
60 g hazelnuts
60 g vegan butter, at room temperature
6 tbsp sugar
3 tsp ground cinnamon
2 pinches ground cardamom
1 pinch ground cloves

For the dough, mix the flour and salt in a bowl. Crumble the yeast, mix with the sugar and add to the bowl. In a saucepan, heat the vegan butter together with the oat milk until the butter melts, then add to the dry ingredients. Mix and then knead everything into a soft and smooth dough. Cover the dough with a damp cloth and leave to rise for at least 2 hours (or overnight).

Dust the work surface with a little flour and roll out the dough to a 1-cm thickness. For the filling, grind the nuts and mix with all the remaining ingredients. Spread the dough with the nut and butter filling, then roll it up and cut into between six and eight scroll-shaped buns. Place the buns in a greased ovenproof dish and bake in a convection oven at 190°C for 30–35 minutes. If using an Omnia, this takes about 10–15 minutes longer on a medium heat.

EGGLESS EGG WASH
Yeast-leavened pastries look particularly beautiful when they are brushed with an egg wash just before baking. The vegan version I like to use is apricot jam, which I heat briefly and mix with a little soya cream. Alternatively, soya cream with a little ground turmeric and a liquid sweetener works quite well.

Cranberry nut bar

This nut bar makes the perfect between-meal snack. It's also good for strenuous activity, whether you're exercising your brain or going on a long hike.

100 g hazelnuts

150 g shelled pistachio nuts

100 g sunflower seeds

80 g dried cranberries

Zest of ½ orange

160 ml rice syrup

½ tsp ground cinnamon

¼ tsp ground star anise

¼ tsp ground cloves

2 pinches freshly grated nutmeg

2 pinches ground cardamom

1 pinch salt

Chop the nuts and pistachios with a large knife and roast them with the sunflower seeds in a non-stick frying pan. Add the remaining ingredients and allow the mixture to caramelise while stirring constantly. Pour the mixture into a square baking tin (about 20 × 20 cm), press well with a silicone scraper or spatula to compact and refrigerate overnight. The next day, cut into bars with a sharp knife. The bars will keep for about three weeks in the fridge.

SPREADS, DIPS AND SAUCES

I've probably never eaten as much bread as I did while on the road. It's just the thing for a quick snack between meals. Of course, bread is always better when eaten with a variety of delicious spreads and dips. I prefer to make them myself with the little stick blender I keep on the van. This chapter shows you how to make the spreads, dips and sauces we used on a weekly basis in our four-wheeled home.

Sweet potato spread

My love of sweet potatoes is common knowledge. They have an incredible aromatic flavour, especially when baked. So, if you're after a recipe for a new spread, you should definitely try this one.

SERVES 2

1 medium sweet potato

200 g cooked chickpeas

Juice and zest of 1 lemon

1 tbsp tahini

3 tbsp olive oil

1 tsp sweetener of choice

1 clove garlic

¼ tsp ground caraway

¼ tsp salt

Pepper

Thoroughly wash and dry the unpeeled sweet potato. Prick several times with a fork and then bake at 200°C for about 40 minutes, until tender. Or bake in the Omnia oven for one hour at the highest temperature. Then peel and blend together with all the other ingredients in a blender or food processor, or with a stick blender until creamy. Serve lukewarm with bread or crispbread.

WHY TAHINI IS CRUCIAL
A good tahini, or white sesame paste, is really important for the flavour and consistency of this spread. It should be light and runny. The best tahini is often found in shops selling Turkish or Middle-Eastern foods.

Tofu and herb dip

Vegan cream cheese is typically made from cashews. Personally, I often find this to be too time-consuming for me because the nuts have to be soaked first. My tofu dip is less complicated. (Pictured opposite)

MAKES 350 ML (1 JAR)

200 g regular tofu

2 cloves garlic

2 tbsp olive oil

Juice of ½ lemon

1 tbsp apple cider vinegar

1 dash plant-based milk

½ tsp salt

½ bunch chives

Pepper

Blend all the ingredients with a stick blender until creamy. You can also add some sun-dried tomatoes if you like. The dip works best as an accompaniment for bread and roasted vegetables.

Lemon hummus

It's no secret that I love lemon. Lemon zest is also wonderful in savoury spreads. I was inspired by the classic hummus recipe for this dip.

MAKES 350 ML (1 JAR)

250 g cooked chickpeas

2 tbsp tahini

3 tbsp olive oil

1 clove garlic

1 tsp sweetener of choice

Juice and zest of 1 lemon

½ tsp salt

½ tsp smoked paprika

2 pinches ground caraway

Pepper

Cold water, as needed

Blend all the ingredients in a blender or food processor, or with a stick blender until smooth. Add cold water if necessary to give the spread the desired creamy consistency.

Pistachio pesto

Pistachio pesto is a Sicilian version of pesto that has always been purely vegan. It often just consists of two ingredients: pistachio nuts and oil.

MAKES 250 ML (I JAR WITH SCREW-TOP LID)

80 g chopped pistachio nuts

25 g fresh basil

100 ml olive oil

15 g yeast flakes

20 g toasted pine nuts

I clove garlic

Juice of ½ lemon

Salt and pepper

Make the pesto by blending all the ingredients with a stick blender, seasoning to taste. Transfer to an airtight jar and cover with more olive oil. This pesto will keep for a fortnight in the fridge and can be frozen.

Peanut and ginger sauce

This sauce is a true all-rounder and goes well with many Asian-inspired dishes. It tastes particularly good with bowl dishes combining many different ingredients. (Pictured opposite)

1½ tbsp peanut butter

3 tbsp soya cream

5 tbsp soya yoghurt

½-cm length fresh ginger

I clove garlic

I tsp date syrup

Use a blender or food processor, or a stick blender to blend all the ingredients to a smooth and creamy sauce.

Four tofu marinades

I often hear that a lot of people just don't like tofu. I firmly believe that it's because they still haven't found the right way of using it as a suitable marinade. Here are some interesting ways to use tofu involving four delicious tofu marinades, made by simply mixing together all the ingredients.

HONEY MUSTARD

1 ½ tsp pear concentrate
2 tsp mustard
1 ½ tsp rapeseed oil
1 ½ tsp garlic powder
½ tsp smoked paprika
½ tsp salt

SWEET 'N SOUR

1 ½ tsp rapeseed oil
1 ½ tsp sambal oelek
2 tsp dark balsamic vinegar
1 tsp pear concentrate
½ tsp garlic powder
1 ½ tsp flour of choice

PESTO ROSSO

2 tsp dried Italian herbs
½ tsp salt
2 tsp olive oil
1 tsp tomato purée
½ tsp garlic powder
1 tsp pear concentrate

CHEESY TAHINI

2 tsp tahini
1 tsp pear concentrate
3 tsp yeast flakes
1 tsp truffle oil
1 tsp salt

For 100 g regular tofu, squeeze well to remove the moisture, cut into cubes and soak in the marinade, coating well. Transfer to an airtight container and leave to steep overnight in the fridge. Then bake in the oven at 200°C for 20 minutes until crispy or sauté in a frying pan with rapeseed oil.

Yoghurt and tahini dip

This dip doesn't need much chopping and blending, but it tastes delicious every time. It goes well with roasted vegetables and rice dishes, and can be used as a condiment for sandwiches and burgers.

2 cloves garlic

300 g soya yoghurt

75 g tahini

2 tbsp lemon juice

1 tsp pear concentrate (or other sweetener)

Salt and pepper

Press the garlic and mix with the remaining ingredients to make the dip. This dip is perfect for roasted vegetables and as a condiment for wraps, burgers, rissoles and falafel.

Apple butter

Apple butter is a delicious alternative to jam as a spread for bread. You definitely need a lot of time and lots of apples to make it. I devised this recipe when we rescued a whole box of already somewhat wrinkly specimens. And all I can say is that I would do it again every time.

MAKES 500 ML (1 LARGE JAR WITH SCREW-TOP LID)

1 kg apples

100 ml apple juice

70 g sugar

Juice and zest of ½ lemon

1 tsp ground cinnamon

1 pinch ground cloves

1 pinch salt

Peel, core and cut the apples into bite-sized pieces and cook them together with the apple juice in a large saucepan on a medium heat for 30 minutes until soft. Remove from the heat and purée. Mix in the remaining ingredients and return to the heat. Cook down, stirring constantly, until the apple butter caramelises, turning brown and thick. The longer apple butter is cooked, the tastier it becomes.

Pour the hot apple butter into a sterilised jar and seal. It will keep for several weeks in the fridge. Apple butter is great as a spread, in porridge or combined with yoghurt and granola.

Recipe index

Acknowledgements

My deepest thanks go to my partner Chris for joining me on this incredible van life adventure. Not only did you eat your way through all the recipes and rate them honestly, but you also so often cleared up the mess I made in the kitchen and served as a hand model for the photographs. I promise you from now on that we'll enjoy our food warm more often, and that I won't always set our meal times according to the best light conditions.

Although we travel as a couple, there are many virtual passengers who share our travels with us who I also must thank. We share all our adventures on Instagram under @aniahimsa with the loyal community of followers who have accompanied us and shown their support for the process involved in creating this cookbook right from the beginning. Without you, this trip would not be possible. Thank you for buying so many copies of my first book *Iss dich grün!* ('Eat Your Greens!') and for still sending me photos of dishes you cook every day. I hope you enjoy *Vegan Camper Van Cooking* as much as I did.

I would also like to give thanks to my family and all our loved ones who we've left behind. It's nice that we can also keep in touch from a distance. Thank you all for letting me go and sharing our happiness as we live out our dream.

I would also thank Camperfabrik. Without you — Samuel, Julia and the team — our four-wheeled home could never have been so perfect. You lovingly worked on Fava, right down to the smallest detail, and made all our ideas a reality, no matter how insane they sounded. Thank you for investing so much time and effort.

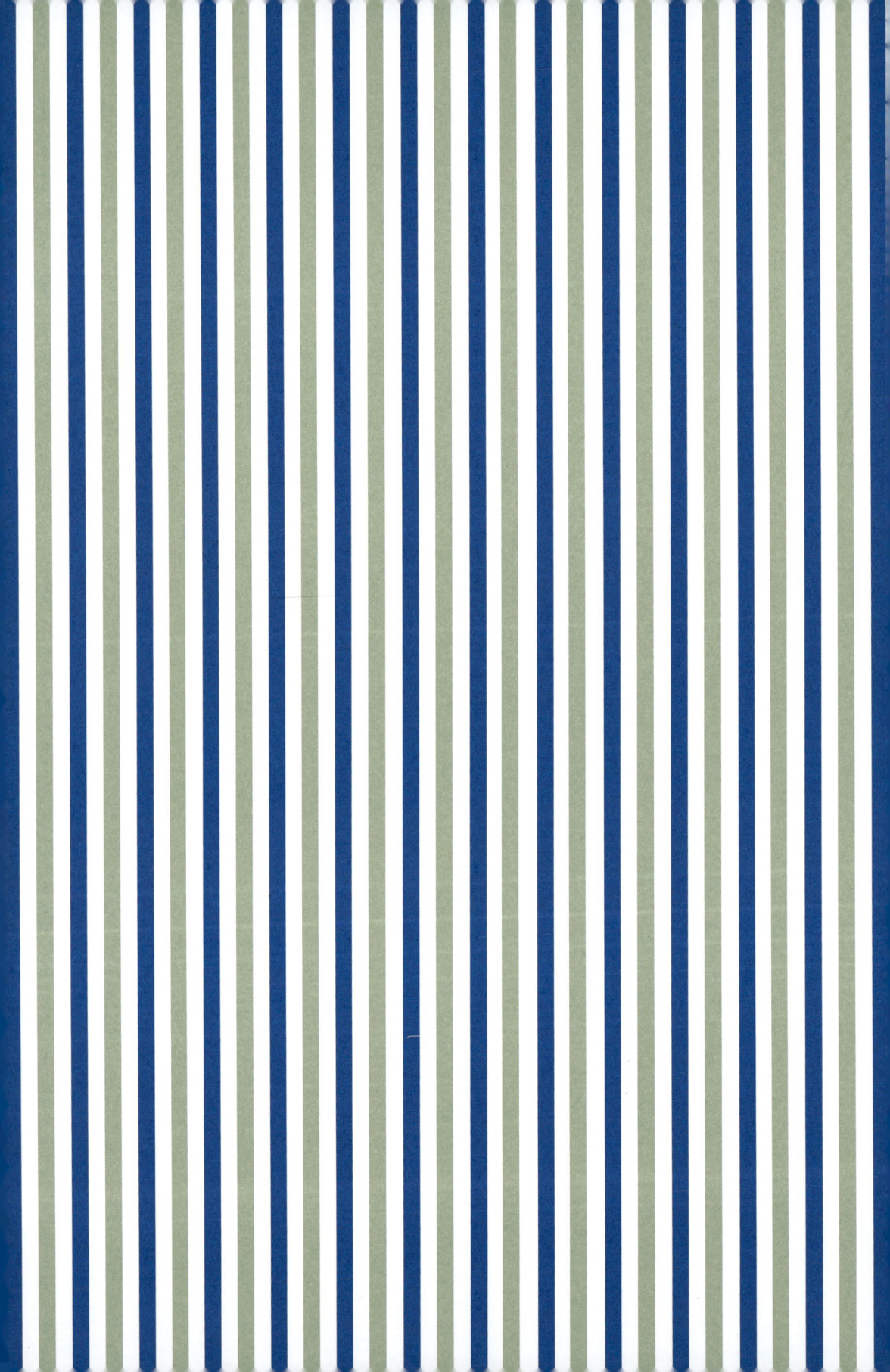